REPARATION
A SPIRITUAL JOURNEY

MARIA HALL

Copyright ©, Maria Hall, 2015
ISBN: 978-0-473-33680-6

All rights reserved. No part of this work may be reproduced or transmitted in any form or by any means, electronic or mechanical, except for the purpose of reviewing or promotion.

Published 2015 by
Haven Publishing

www.mariahallwriter.com

Cover design by YOCLA designs
Cover photograph by N H C Abbott

Disclaimer

All the events in this book, REPARATION, A SPIRITUAL JOURNEY, are true and accurate according to the author. The names of various individuals have been changed to protect their identity. The opinions expressed in this book are those of the author.

Table of Contents

Chapter 1 In Confession 1

Chapter 2 The T'ree Vows 13

Chapter 3 Psychological Scrutiny.................. 18

Chapter 4 A Double Life 25

Chapter 5 Nuns by Candlelight 33

Chapter 6 Bully in the Classroom.................. 40

Chapter 7 A Testing Time 46

Chapter 8 Life in the Oasis 52

Chapter 9 Mary's Submission 62

Chapter 10 Experimenting with Change 68

Chapter 11 At Bedtime 74

Chapter 12 Danger.. 81

Chapter 13 The Retreat.................................. 90

Chapter 14 A Mother's Fears 100

Chapter 15 Yellow Daffodils....................... 107

Chapter 16 Apparitions and Ecstasies 117

Chapter 17 The Pact 127

Chapter 18 The Village................................ 134

Chapter 19 The Carmelite Nuns 147

Chapter 20 The Abbey................................. 160

Chapter 21 A Personal Attack	169
Chapter 22 Pomp and Pageantry	180
Chapter 23 Nightshift	189
Chapter 24 1 Corinthians	200
Chapter 25 Gossip and Lies	211
Chapter 26 Alone in my Room	219
Chapter 27 The Vision	228
Chapter 28 Letting Go	234
Chapter 29 Conflict at Home	241
Chapter 30 Back to School	249
Chapter 31 Becoming Human	258
Chapter 32 Togetherness	270
Acknowledgements	279
Glossary	281

Chapter 1
In Confession

Mother screamed with horror – as I expected she would – before grabbing her inhaler. She was having an asthma attack. I felt dreadful.

"I'm suffering just like the Sorrowful Mother," she sobbed. "All my children are going to hell and you're no different from the rest of them. Sometimes I wish I'd never married."

I remained quiet. I had heard it all so many times before but the difference, this time, was that I was the cause of her grief.

"You watch! I'll be dead soon and then you'll all be sorry you didn't listen to your mother."

She glanced at Dad who was drying the lunch dishes, a look of disgust on her face. She always blamed Dad for any weaknesses and shortcomings in her children.

I went to my room and closed the door. I needed to be alone. Four short years had slipped by and now, at twenty-four, I was changed beyond recognition – physically, emotionally.

It all began one Saturday morning. Having confessed my sins, none of which were serious, I was waiting for Father McSweeney to give me absolution.

"Have ya ever t'ought of becomin' a nun, Maria?" he whispered.

His words resounded in my head as I stared at the black curtain in the confessional box. I'd just received Jesus in Holy Communion and I was feeling happy. I liked Jesus. He was a good man.

"Yes," I whispered.

I was being polite. Actually, I only started thinking about it right then.

"Jesus needs generous souls, Maria. He asks us to trust him. Do ya trust Jesus?"

"Yes, I do, Father."

I leant into the curtain, not wanting to miss a word, while noting Father McSweeney's Irish accent was different from my grandmother's – an accent that couldn't possibly be from Belfast. So was Father McSweeney from Dublin? Or from…

"Do you love Jesus with all ya heart and soul?"

He was interrupting my thoughts.

"Yes, I do, Father."

"That's greet. And ya want to please Jesus, don't ya?"

"Yes, Father, of course I do."

"A religious vocation is a very special t'ing, Maria; a gift from God. A nun takes t'ree vows, ya know: vows of poverty, chastity and obedience. Those vows will lead her on the path to sanctity. Do you understand?"

Mother was coughing at the back of the church, probably wondering why I was taking so long and, therefore, what I might be confessing. However, Father McSweeney was doing the talking and I thought he should hurry up and finish.

"Yes, Father."

"The Church needs religious vocations to continue its mission to spread the gospel of Christ all over the world. The Church needs young women just like you."

What was Father leading up to? He had never spoken to me like this before.

"Can I ring ya later todey? I'd like to arrange a meetin' with ya, to discuss your religious vocation."

My religious vocation? What vocation? I'd never seriously thought of having a vocation until that very moment. I dreamed of boys, of love and marriage, and of living on a houseboat. Someday, there would be a soundproof room in a sprawling bungalow where I could play the piano and sing opera at the top of my voice – without disturbing the neighbours.

Father McSweeney had cast out his net and caught me off-guard. Nevertheless, that was what he was meant to do, wasn't he? To be a fisher of men? Jesus asked that of him.

He had been quite clever setting me up to say a whole lot of 'yeses', one after another. Did all priests operate like that in an effort to get young people to enter the convent and the priesthood? I felt slightly suspicious.

Father McSweeney absolved me from my sins and gave me some penance to recite. I left the confessional and walked across to one of the pews on the other side of the church. I knelt and said my penance: one 'Our Father', three 'Hail Marys' and one 'Glory be'. Penance was always the same when Father McSweeney was dispensing it.

As the rest of the family filed in and out of the confessional box, I thought about the idea of dedicating my life to God as a nun. Somehow, the sacrifice, the commitment and the practice of Christian virtue seemed appealing. I wanted to do something worthwhile with my life and I realised there was really nothing stopping me. I was a believer and I loved God. I knew the only obstacles were selfishness, worldliness or weakness – and Father McSweeney was challenging me not to indulge in any of those shortcomings.

The parish church of Our Lady of Fatima in Auckland, New Zealand, was a very poor example of a house of God. It was cheap – constructed from two American Nissen Army huts dating back to World War II – and barely adequate for any kind of religious service, even in 1974. But at least the congregation wasn't burdened with the expense of a smart, new church; at least, not then.

Neither the architecture nor the furnishings of the church offered the believer any kind of spiritual inspiration, other than a sense of poverty. A war was raging among the parishioners – to keep Jesus in the manger, or provide Him with a building more worthy of His kingly status.

My Faith wasn't dependent on inspiration from cathedral ceilings, stained glass windows or marble statues. My Faith came from within: from my heart and mind, my Catholic upbringing, my maternal grandmother and, most especially, from Mother.

Father Eustace McSweeney, Father Flanaghan Lynch and Brother John, the three Capuchin monks who administered the church, were new to the parish. They had only recently arrived in New Zealand from Ireland, and we had just moved into the neighbourhood and joined the parish, too. They had impressed us with their fervour and prayerfulness from the very first Mass we attended. Their homilies challenged us to be more authentic, more committed to Christian values.

The monks wore traditional long Franciscan robes, with bare feet and sandals. During the six weeks of Lent, leading up to Easter, they shaved the crown of their heads in a tonsure and grew beards, as symbols of sacrifice and penance. Their body fat visibly reduced due to fasting. Such displays of religious fervour among the clergy of Auckland were extremely rare, if not unheard of, and we watched in awe.

As Dad drove us home from church that morning, I gazed out the car window, thinking about the conversation with Father McSweeney. The more I pondered, the more I realised I wanted to make the ultimate sacrifice too, and give my life to God as a nun.

As the car turned into our driveway, I decided to share my news with the family – the news that I had a religious vocation – and after breakfast seemed like an appropriate time. There was no need to make a fuss during the meal. I was a bit like Dad in that respect. I liked peace and calm. Physically, I was like Dad too, tall and lean. Mother, on the other hand, was a petite woman, with a curvaceous figure. Her once blonde hair had darkened and was going grey but her diminutive size and soft colouring could be deceptive. I didn't look anything like her.

Wholemeal toast and homemade marmalade didn't taste quite as delicious as usual that morning. My life was about to change dramatically but I knew I was ready for change. I was more than ready. I was twenty years old and still living at home, still being treated like a child because Mother took her responsibilities as a parent very seriously. She was making sure my brothers and I were leading Catholic lives and that we didn't fall into "dangerous occasions of sin", as she put it.

We weren't allowed to go flatting before we got married and we most certainly weren't allowed to stay out all night, lose our virginity or experiment with sex in any way. In fact, the word "sex" was never used at home. Mother's favourite words were "abstinence", "self-denial", and "squashing the appetites of the flesh". And I believed every word she said.

While we lived under our parents' roof, we had to obey all the rules of the Catholic Church as well as Mother's old-fashioned ones. We recited prayers in the car every morning on the way to Mass and back. We said Grace before and after meals, the Angelus at noon, and the Rosary after dinner. We fell asleep each night muttering a collection of prayers that Mother had taught us from a very young age. We obeyed the Ten Commandments and the Six Commandments of the Church, and we practised charity and all the other Christian virtues, even donating our pocket money to missionary priests working in Africa and India.

Furthermore, Mother gave many of our possessions, including the television and radio, to poor migrant workers who had arrived in Auckland from the Pacific Islands. Apparently, their needs were greater than ours.

When Dad and my brothers, Damian and Joe, finished eating breakfast and left the dining room, I saw an opportunity to speak to Mother on my own. I wanted to talk to her first. She was my mother and I loved her dearly.

She was loading the dishwasher as I stacked the dirty dishes on the orange Formica bench of the servery.

"I think I'm going to become a nun," I said, avoiding eye contact.

Outside, the water in the swimming pool was shimmering softly in the morning light. I stood there, staring.

Mother didn't answer. Had she heard me? My family wasn't very good with words, myself included. I had to fill the silence, quickly.

"Father McSweeney spoke to me in confession this morning. He thinks I'd be a good nun."

Mother stopped loading the dishwasher. "You, a nun?"

She was fidgeting with her yellow and white checked apron, neatly tied at the waist. I picked up the butter dish and marmalade, walked around the servery and into the kitchen, into Mother's zone, and opened the fridge.

"Yes! Why not? You've always encouraged us to do everything for God."

She couldn't argue with that statement. I put the butter and marmalade on the top shelf and closed the fridge door before turning to face her.

"But not a nun," she said.

"What's the big deal?"

"Eddie! Come here!" she called to Dad. She sounded anxious. I hadn't expected that. I walked back into the dining room and continued clearing the table, wondering what to say next.

"You're meant to be a mother," she said. "You're a born mother. Of all my children you're the most suited to becoming a parent."

That was news to me.

"From the time you were a little tot you've always helped me around the house."

"So?" I shrugged.

"Eddie! I need you!" she called again. "Where are you?"

"I don't understand what all the fuss is about. It makes perfect sense to me," I said.

A minute or two later Dad strolled into the dining room. He was smiling, which was usual for Dad. Damian and Joe followed him in. They had overheard the conversation and seemed mildly surprised – perhaps even pleased at my news.

The conversation about my religious vocation continued on and off throughout the day over cups of tea and plates of food. As the hours slipped by, I waited patiently for Father McSweeney to ring me, as he'd arranged, but he didn't. Feeling a little deflated I went to bed at 9.45pm.

An hour later Dad woke me – Father McSweeney was on the phone. Never having had a private conversation with a priest before, except in confession and that didn't count, it seemed very odd to talk to him, especially since it was so late.

By the following morning, Mother had had twenty-four hours to think about my religious vocation.

"What on earth is Father McSweeney doing, ringing my daughter so late?"

She was annoyed but that wasn't uncommon. Her question was directed at Dad. I explained that he had apologised for ringing so late. He had been delayed in a meeting that had continued too long. It wasn't his fault.

"I'm the mother of this family. I know what you're meant to do in life, my girl! Why is this priest interfering in my family?"

No one answered. I looked over at Dad. Usually I tried to follow Dad's example of calm and moderation, but I was a girl, too, just like Mother. I identified with her – with her intense emotion. Occasionally Dad got frustrated with me and threatened to send me to my bedroom but, on that particular day, I felt composed and focused, despite the nervous excitement swirling inside. Considering the importance that religion had in the family, I found Mother's objections unreasonable and hypocritical.

Moreover, the spirit of self-sacrifice was very alive in our family. Mother's first husband was killed during World War II, on Anzac Day, April 25 1945, only a few days before the war in Europe ended. Overnight the young bride became a solo mother. Four years later she married my dad, a veteran soldier of the same war. Dad knew he was lucky to have survived five long years in the infantry, in campaigns fought in North Africa and Italy. He marvelled at his good fortune, thanking God for protecting him when all his mates had been killed.

Throughout our childhood we were reminded of that war, of that loss and sacrifice. Mother was anxious to keep alive the memory of her first husband for the sake of her first born, and for her own sake, and our sakes. We were a family of eight, with three girls and three boys. I was their youngest daughter.

Dad's own stories of that war were never-ending. The millions of flies, the constant digging of trenches, the shell shock, the shrapnel, the fear, the brutality of hand to hand combat, and the exhilaration of fighting for a just cause. He recalled the good times, too, such as yachting on the Nile, leave weekends in England, and the chance to visit his father's family in Northern Ireland. The spirit of sacrifice and service was deeply embedded in the psyche of every member of our family.

"Your grandmother never encouraged any of us to become nuns," Mother said. "She thought the nuns were bad-tempered and uncharitable."

"Well, I won't be bad-tempered or uncharitable," I replied. "I'll be a happy nun. I don't understand why you're so upset. I thought you'd be pleased. You brought us up to give of our best *and* to give our best to God. I'm following through on that training."

Unlike some Catholic families, we had no proud history of religious vocations. Dad's family were 'Sunday Catholics' and even Mass on Sunday was skipped, without a qualm, if something else was on. But religion played a vital role in Mother's family, even though her father had converted to Catholicism only after the death of his baby daughter. Barely able to contain his grief, he consoled himself with the thought that he could be reunited with her in heaven one day. And, if a change of religious affiliation could effect that dream, then, so be it.

I looked over at Dad and tried to read his face.

"I'll boil the kettle," he said, stroking his greying beard. "Who's for coffee?"

"Yes, please," Damian and Joe shouted from the lounge.

"No, thanks," Mother said.

Mother had breathed God's love into every cell of my being from the moment of my conception. I knew I loved God. I was a believer. Also, I was available. I didn't have a boyfriend at the time – my heart had taken a beating two years before, and I was far from carefree when it came to romantic attachments.

Over the next few weeks, I informed the extended family of my decision. Some, like Mother, expressed apprehension. They knew quite a few nuns who'd been damaged by years of psychological abuse at the hands of their superiors.

Of course, I didn't understand. I had no experience of such things.

With support from Dad, Damian, Joe and Father McSweeney I remained committed to the idea of a religious vocation and, eventually, Mother's attitude softened.

Chapter 2
The T'ree Vows

"Do ya t'ink Jesus is calling ya to himself, Maria?" Father McSweeney asked.

My feet dug into the carpet as I sat in a small meeting room in the presbytery. Father McSweeney was interviewing me. He was sitting in a tan upholstered armchair and I was on the matching sofa. His papers were scattered across a cheap brown Formica coffee table. The room didn't feel homely. It was obvious that only men lived in the presbytery.

I nodded my head in agreement, listening intently.

"A religious vorcation is a very special t'ing; a blessing from God," he said, enunciating each word perfectly, as was his way. "God doesn't give a religious vorcation to everyone, Maria."

His voice trembled with fervour. I searched his face, trying to read his thoughts. Beads of perspiration glistened on his high forehead. His fine hair was swished back with Brylcreem, not a hair out of place. It was a hot day. Dressed in thick Franciscan robes the heat must have been unbearable.

"As I'm sure ya know, there are t'ree vows. The first vow is poverty, which enables us to share in the poverty of Christ who became poor for our sake: poor in fact and poor in spirit. Our treasure is in heaven with God, Maria."

His piercing blue eyes were boring into me.

"The second vow is chastity. Chastity frees the heart in a unique and special way so dat it may be more inflamed with the love of God and all mankind. In dis way a nun is able to serve God with all her heart and soul and carry out apostolic works."

Stealing a glance around the room I checked out every corner. This was the first time I had stepped inside a presbytery. My eyes settled on a pink plastic rose decorating a white plaster statue of Mary on the sideboard. I shifted my gaze back to Father McSweeney and made eye contact again.

"The t'ird vow is obedience. Obedience implies full and utter surrender of one's will as a sacrifice to God and, in so doing, we are united permanently to God's hooly will. With God's hooly grace, not'ing is impossible."

Father licked his lips, his mouth dry. I was surprised he hadn't offered me a cup of tea or a glass of water, but I reminded myself that this was not a social visit.

"As gold is refined and purified so are we tried and tested. Our response must be unwavering."

I let the words sink in, focussing on the crucifix behind him. Jesus had died on the cross to save us, to open the gates of heaven. His sacrifice was proof of God's infinite love. Following Jesus had consequences. I could expect to fall under the weight of the cross but, after Calvary, there would be a resurrection. There would be gifts and fruits of the Holy Spirit. Gifts of love, patience, understanding, joy, peace and wisdom.

"So, Maria, your next task is to choose a Religious Order."

It seemed I'd passed the first interview. I was surprised it was that easy. There was no probing, testing or analysing. He didn't have a clue who I was and that didn't seem to matter to him.

Did my strengths and weaknesses, my hopes and dreams, mean nothing at all as a prospective nun? I was confused but hid my concern. God knew I loved Him and I was confident He would look after me.

I guessed Father McSweeney was judging me on other things. He greeted my family at Mass every morning. He visited our home in a well-to-do neighbourhood. He saw a large crucifix and holy water font hanging in the front entrance, and a baby grand piano and elegant furniture in the lounge – fruits of hard work, ambition, and success.

"How will I go about choosing a Religious Order?" I asked.

He handed me a pile of brochures advertising different Orders and suggested that I ring them up and visit them. Then he sent me on my way.

I walked home, satisfied. Billowing white clouds were racing across the blue sky. It was blowing a stiff twenty-knot sou'wester, a typical Auckland summer's day.

The buckle on my wooden-soled sandals broke so I took them off and continued barefoot. It was 1974 and I looked like any other music student at Auckland University. John Lennon glasses sat on my nose and my hair was brushed into a thick

Afro. The flowery pattern on my tight yellow trousers was faded, the stripy T-shirt and the olive green jacket also suitably faded. A Pro-Life slogan printed on the back of the jacket and a string of handmade Rosary beads hanging around my neck were the only signs bearing witness to my Faith.

My thoughts focused on Jesus: the Good Shepherd, the Light of the World, the Way, the Truth and the Life. The parables were wonderful stories of God's infinite love. I modelled my life on that of the Good Samaritan. I was ready for whatever challenge Jesus might send my way.

In many ways I was a typical young woman of that time: liberated, educated and confident. Travelling the world or having a career in music were both attractive possibilities but the voice inside my head was very persistent. It reminded me of Jesus' call to leave everything – home, family, career, possessions – and to follow Him.

The concept of religious vocation appealed to my sense of purity of intent, of sacrifice and service. I needed something to pour my energy into. I needed a direction, a purpose, something to feel passionate about. I needed someone to love and I decided *that* someone would be God and the whole human race.

My view of women was limited, based on the model of Catholic women my mother befriended through her charity work. These women were exhausted and depressed from child-bearing.

Mother's health had deteriorated too. She relied on Dad to calm her nerves, ease her shoulder pain, and cool her hot flushes. The once dynamic woman had become an asthmatic a few years earlier, shortly after her own mother died. Asthma attacks, combined with bronchitis, exacerbated her natural inclination to fear as she convinced herself she was going to die.

Prednisone-fuelled sleeplessness dominated her nights, laced with haunted dreams. She would wake, sobbing, and then accuse us of "not caring enough". Lying in bed, day after day, she wallowed in self-pity, driven by the knowledge that three of her children had left home and were not living up to her high expectations. She comforted herself with prayer, which may have helped her soul but did little for her health. The once loving, vivacious wife and mother had become a frustrated and angry invalid.

Dad was a wonderful nurse – patient, kind, unflappable – and my brothers and I tried to follow his example, despite the difficulties, despite the insults. Sometimes, after a six-week bout in bed, we would return home at the end of the day to find Mother in the kitchen. Life would return to normal for two or three weeks.

Being the youngest daughter, and the only daughter still at home, I identified with Mother more than my brothers did. There were times when I desperately wanted to get away from her, but I wasn't a rebel and so I didn't leave home. In making her happiness my focus, my own dreams quietly faded. That is until Father McSweeney cornered me in confession that Saturday morning, changing my life forever.

Chapter 3
Psychological Scrutiny

I studied the material supplied by Father McSweeney and visited various Religious Orders based in Auckland. Father McSweeney assured me that I would feel a special connection to one of them. I just needed to put in time, effort and prayer, and God would do the rest.

However, I didn't feel a special bond with any of them although I could appreciate the good work they did. Nonetheless, I was very certain of one small point: I was never going to prance around in a prissy little habit with a neat blue veil on my head, posing like a goodie-goodie, a bride of Christ. That image made me cringe. I was an ordinary girl in the real world and I wanted to stay that way, serving others in Christ's name, and sharing His endless love.

I had already completed a Diploma of Teaching so it made sense to join a teaching Order. The Order of the Sacred Heart nuns at Baradene College, where I had attended school for six years in my teens, seemed the obvious choice.

The word Baradene is derived from the name of the French woman who founded the worldwide teaching Order in the aftermath of the French Revolution, Saint Madeleine Sophie Barat (1779-1865). She was known for her virtue, and especially her wisdom, charity, humility and prayerfulness. She believed in the education of girls, the formation of their characters and the guidance of their souls. She set up schools to achieve that for the rich and poor alike. Her views on education were profound and enlightened.

When I told Father McSweeney my decision to join the Sacred Heart nuns, he shook his head in disapproval.

"They've abandoned the wearing of their religious habit," he said. "The habit is a sign of consecration to God, for all the world to see."

My eyes wandered over the folds of his Franciscan robe which brushed his sandaled feet. Secretly I had to admit that his religious dress was rather special. But a small audience had joined us outside the church and I was feeling brave.

"I don't think that matters, Father," I replied. "Vatican Council II encourages priests and nuns to change, to get with it, to modernise."

We locked eyes.

"Yes, but not to forget their roots, their sacred history, the spirit of their holy founders and foundresses," he said, knotting his brow in frustration.

"Just because they don't wear their traditional habit anymore doesn't mean they've forgotten the spirit of their founders and foundresses."

I knew he and I would never agree on this subject. The Sacred Heart nuns looked like ordinary women, a crucial thing in their favour for me. They were trying to be modern and relevant, and I was modern and wanted to be relevant.

Before the Provincial Superior of the Australasian branch of the Sacred Heart Order gave me permission to enter the Order, I was summoned to Baradene College to undergo a psychological assessment. Naturally I felt a bit nervous as I pressed the bell at the front door, waiting for someone to appear. My hands were perspiring. They always did when I was tense.

A couple of minutes later Sister Gertrude opened the door and led me into a formal lounge where a priest was waiting to interview me. He was the psychologist.

"Pleased to meet you, Maria," he said, shaking my hand. "I'm Father Jim. Call me Jim. Take a seat."

"Thank you, Father."

"I'll leave you two to get on with your meeting," Sister Gertrude said before heading towards the door and closing it softly behind her.

"Call me Jim, remember?" he said, glancing in my direction. He was tall and lean, with longish hair, dressed in a black suit with white clerical collar. He sat down and crossed his legs.

I glanced around the room. It was light, spacious and sparsely furnished with Queen Anne tables and chairs: rather old-fashioned and slightly musty.

I felt relieved that Father Jim seemed relaxed and normal, not at all uptight and formal like Father McSweeney.

Father Jim asked me lots of questions over the next hour, occasionally referring to his papers. Most of the questions were about family, schooling, upbringing and my commitment to Christ. They were logical and straightforward and I thought I answered them well.

I had come to the interview prepared to be mentally and emotionally peeled, chopped and grated but, instead, Father Jim and I were having an intelligent conversation. My confidence was growing. I could sense his approval. I almost called him Jim once or twice.

"Have you ever been in love?" he asked. The question came as a complete surprise.

"Yes," I replied, holding my breath. I had always been 'in love'.

Looking down at the carpet, I recalled the pain of a broken heart. I kept my eyes down, waiting for the next question. It had been so easy so far. Surely, the critical questions, the tough ones, must lie ahead. There would have to be questions about the vow of celibacy, and if I could practise celibacy and control my feelings.

Sexual feelings were natural and normal, but my task now, as an aspiring young nun, was to overcome them somehow. I assumed God would give me the grace to squash them or that He would have mercy on me. He would listen to my prayers and banish those feelings from my body.

My reading about the lives of the great saints spoke of purity of intent, self-denial, trust in God and, in extreme cases, self-flagellation. However, I wasn't planning on whipping myself. That idea was definitely medieval.

Honesty was my best and only option, despite the embarrassment of talking about such things with a stranger. Father Jim was twenty years older than me but he looked relaxed and trendy. As he paused, I stared at him blankly, hoping he couldn't read my thoughts. I was quite good at acting, having studied speech and drama as a teenager.

"Maria, you said you're doing a degree in music at university. Who's your favourite composer?" he asked, shuffling his papers noisily; too noisily.

Keep still, don't fidget, I told myself.

"The Romantic composers. Beethoven, Tchaikovsky, Debussy. And some from the late Romantic and early twentieth century. Wagner, Gustave Holtz, Alban Berg. I have lots of favourites. And, of course, I love Santana and Osibisa. And Andrae Crouch and the Disciples."

Keep the conversation going, Maria.

"Have you heard of Andrae Crouch?" I asked aloud. "He sings black gospel music. It's really great."

I wondered why he'd sidestepped the crucial questions, seemingly letting me off the hook, making it easy for me. Or was it a trick? Was he going to return to the subject of chastity? Or masturbation? Was he going to ask me if I was a virgin? And when I said "yes", would he ask me how I could be sure I could give up the act of making love forever when I'd never experienced it?

"No, I haven't," he said. "Do you play the piano?"

"Yes, I do but I enjoy singing most of all."

"That's nice," he replied, shuffling his papers again. "Well, Maria, I think that about covers it for today. There's really no need for any further questions."

"Oh, really?"

"Yes. That's it. All done."

We smiled at each other. Could he read my thoughts? My relief? Was he pleased the interview was over, too?

We stood up, shook hands and walked across the lounge together. My long skirt rustled softly with each footstep. I was almost at the door, almost out of reach of his scrutiny. Could he hear my heart thumping?

Sister Gertrude was hovering in the foyer, two inches off the ground. A tall, serene woman.

"Father Jim, can you wait one moment?" she asked politely. "I've got something to give you."

He nodded. She had an envelope in her hand. *A donation*, I thought. Of course, he had to be paid for his time and effort. I wondered how much money an interview like this was worth.

"Maria, you're free to go, dear. We'll be in touch. Sister Amy will ring you."

"Thank you Sister. Thank you Father."

Stepping outside, into the bright light, I was conscious of the missed opportunity of learning something from him or even learning something about myself. Unanswered questions were buzzing in my head. Did it matter? Did it matter that I felt both relief and regret?

It seemed too easy that I could be accepted into the Sacred Heart Order based on one interview. But it was the 1970s. The Church was modernizing. Priests and nuns were abandoning their Religious Orders in record numbers and new enrolments had decreased dramatically. Any prospective candidates were, therefore, keenly welcomed.

Chapter 4
A Double Life

On Saturday afternoon, 24th February 1976, my parents and I drove into the sweeping tree-lined driveway at Loreto Hall, a Catholic Teachers Training College. It was situated in one of Auckland's more exclusive suburbs.

I had been given permission to join the small community of nuns of the Sacred Heart Order who administered the College. It was disappointing not to be going to the large community of nuns at Baradene College, a place that was familiar to me from my school days, but that decision hadn't been mine to make.

During the previous eighteen months, I had been frustrated by a delay imposed by the Sacred Heart Order which required me to finish my Bachelor of Music course at university and spend a year studying theology and scripture. With all the intensity and impatience of youth, I struggled to slow down and bide time. But now, at twenty-two, I was allowed to move on to the next phase and enter the Order.

Dad parked the car outside the main house, a rambling, single-storey, brick and tile bungalow. The only other building on the property had been purpose-built, with lecture rooms downstairs and accommodation for student boarders upstairs.

"Mr and Mrs Hall, I presume. Pleased to meet you," Sister said as she stepped forward to greet us.

Four nuns were standing by the front steps, smiling and ready to shake our hands. They introduced themselves one by one.

"Just one suitcase, Maria?" one of them asked, watching Dad empty the boot.

"Yes, that's right. It's a big one but not too heavy," I said, grabbing my school bag and guitar.

I'd packed only one suitcase with my clothes, mostly homemade long skirts and blouses, handmade leather sandals, woollen jerseys, scarves and beanies, a corduroy jacket and a black winter duffle coat – an old favourite. Remembering that a vow of poverty was part of my religious commitment I was taking only the bare essentials: a few favourite music books and records, plus my Bible.

Conscious that my image was a bit too modern for a nun, I'd smoothed down my Afro and given away colourful beads and dangly earrings. I'd even sold my boat, named *Trisha*, a twenty-four-foot trimaran painted sky blue and white.

"Well, that's it, Mr Hall," another Sister said, looking at Dad. "Maria will be fine with us. Don't you worry. We'll look after her."

Dad, Mother and I looked at one another, somewhat surprised. So they weren't inviting my parents inside to have a cup of tea and a chat, or to see my bedroom. This was it, the meet and greet.

"Bye-bye, darling," Dad said, giving me a hug. "Good-bye, Sisters. It's been a pleasure meeting you." He shook hands with each of them.

Mother gave me a hug.

"God bless you all," she said.

I waved as my parents drove away. I had no idea if I would miss them. I'd never been away from home before. Loreto Hall was to be home for an 'initiation year', to experience life in a religious community. I was feeling positive and trusting God. I was good at that.

Three weeks before entering the convent, I had started my first year of teaching at a co-educational state school on the other side of Auckland because I needed to get an important piece of paper: a Teacher's Certificate. Catholic schools were integrated into the government-funded education system and teaching nuns, who were qualified, were paid state salaries, or rather their Religious Order was. The Mother Superior of the Sacred Heart Order was keen for me to get the certificate and be properly qualified before I taught in one of her schools, hence the need for me to teach in a non-Catholic school.

I settled into an upstairs bedroom during that first weekend. The room was small, the mattress on the bed lumpy and saggy. A simple wooden desk and chair occupied one corner at the base of the bed and a wardrobe and hand basin filled the other corner. The wooden floor was bare as were the walls. It was more like a room in a hospital than a convent. Looking out the window at the tree-lined driveway, I felt completely alone for the first time in my life.

I woke early on Monday morning and dressed quickly. I opened my bedroom door and looked along the corridor, hoping to see someone and say a cheerful good morning. But the corridor was empty and all other bedroom doors closed. There wasn't a sound to be heard, neither a squeak nor a sneeze. Not a nun to be seen, nor a student boarder. Obviously, the students were still in bed, all fifteen of them. But the nuns? Surely, they weren't still in bed at seven o'clock?

There was no one in the bathroom or kitchen either. After eating breakfast, I made some sandwiches for lunch before returning to my room to collect my school bag. As I walked downstairs and out the front door, I felt disappointed no one else was around. I was used to a big family, to hustle and bustle, to chatter and chores every minute of every day. However, I had to acknowledge the relief I felt at being away from Mother's wheezing and coughing and gasping for air; away from her panic and fear.

Reddish-brown shingle crunched under my sandals on the driveway. Curved grass borders glistened in the morning light. Blackbirds were singing merrily in the pururi trees, reminding me of four long-haired lads from Liverpool. The freshness of the new day smelt good. I thanked God for the beautiful world and all its people. This was my first day as an aspiring young nun heading off to school, in a secular world that felt pagan, but I was feeling optimistic.

At the corner, I crossed the road and waited for the geography teacher to arrive. He had agreed to give me a lift to school each day, there and back. He had no idea where I lived, and I had no intention of telling him. From this moment I was a first-year teacher by day and an aspiring nun the rest of the time. It was a bit like leading a double life and I could see the absurdity in it.

That day at school was the same as usual, except everything in my world had changed and no one there knew. Once or twice during the day my conscience reminded me of the deceit I was caught up in, as the principal never would have appointed me to the staff if I had presented myself as a trainee nun, although it wasn't my fault. I was doing as instructed by Sister Amy.

Although I was new to teaching, I had already decided that teaching wasn't for me, not long term. Being in control of a room full of noisy students, reprimanding and disciplining them hour after hour, was not enjoyable. I was looking to the future and wondering what else might lie ahead.

At the end of the day I returned to Loreto Hall, feeling inquisitive. What was life like on the College campus? Who were these nuns? The grounds were deserted so I climbed the squeaky wooden stairs to my bedroom, dumped my school bag on the bed and headed to a small kitchen used by the nuns. I hoped that Mavis, the lay custodian who lived on the campus, wouldn't be there. It was an uncharitable thought but Mavis was a tough, cranky spinster with a gruff voice. From the first moment I met her, she had been authoritarian and overbearing, and I had decided to keep as far away from her as possible. I wasn't a naughty student who needed to be bullied and threatened.

I sneaked into the kitchen, and closed the door noiselessly behind me. A few minutes later I left, coffee cup in hand. From the upstairs vantage point in my room, I could see groups of student boarders sitting under the trees beside the tennis courts. Alone, unseen and unheard, I sipped my coffee, wondering about the nuns.

Time was marching on. It was already 4:35 pm. Time to walk up the road and go to Mass. The other nuns at Loreto Hall had attended Mass earlier in the day and I had been told to walk up the road to the convent of the Missionary Sisters and attend Mass there. I walked quickly, not wanting to be late. Mass was due to start at 5:00 pm.

The chapel was empty, but soon filled as the nuns filed in. Everyone was dressed in a knee-length blue habit and matching veil, with a crucifix and chain around the neck. Unlike the Sacred Heart Order, these nuns had opted to continue wearing a religious habit, although the latest version had been modernised.

A small bell rang and a priest walked into the sanctuary. He was a handsome man who looked utterly miserable. He saw me staring into his eyes, yet his eyes remained vacant. I wondered why.

Mass was said in quiet measured tones, without emotion. It was quite a contrast to the noisy ceremonies I was used to with crying babies, squirming toddlers, cranky teenagers and distracted parents.

After Mass all the nuns left the chapel, heads bowed, eyes lowered. They looked like they were in a hurry and I guess their dinner was ready. No one even acknowledged me, which seemed very odd.

Wandering back to Loreto Hall I talked to myself and to God. I hoped He was listening. A short cut through a park brought me back to the old bungalow at Loreto Hall which housed the administration offices, library, chapel, kitchen and dining areas. The lecturers' staffroom became the nuns' lounge each night and I headed there, hoping to find someone. The room was small and cosy, cluttered with books and papers.

The nuns arrived on the dot of six o'clock. A dinner trolley was wheeled in by the kitchen staff, the television turned on. We ate dinner in front of the television, balancing our plates on our laps.

This was my first opportunity to speak to the other nuns in the community. I watched, keen to fit in. Knives and forks were soon busy. World news droned on in the background, stifling any possible conversation. In any case, it was bad manners to speak with one's mouth full.

The nuns looked as tired as I was. I glanced from one to the other, ready to pick up a cue. When everyone had finished the first course, plates were stacked, and pudding bowls were filled with rhubarb pie and whipped cream. Food had never tasted so scrumptious.

Over mugs of hot coffee furrowed brows relaxed, and eyes softened. A short formal exchange of words ensued about the weather forecast. A trip to the museum was planned for the college students for the following day.

Three of the nuns had been in the Order for twenty years or more. During that time they had seen huge changes. For years they had been clothed in a severe black habit from head to toe, the one I remembered from my school days. Also, when not in the classroom teaching, they had practised a vow of silence. However, those days were gone. Overnight, with the implementation of changes encouraged by Vatican Council II, the nuns were allowed to wear whatever they liked, and they were allowed to talk. I was yet to discover if talking came easily to them. I wondered what it would take before I was included in their conversation.

Chapter 5
Nuns by Candlelight

Each night, immediately after dinner, the television was turned off, the lights dimmed, and a candle lit and placed on the floor between us. It was time for community prayer, with the nuns taking turns to lead. Spontaneous shared prayer was part of the routine and, since there were only five of us, there was plenty of time and opportunity for everyone to be heard.

Leader:
Heavenly Father, we come before You in faith.
Remembering Jesus' words in St John's Gospel chapter 15: 'I am the vine and you are the branches. If a man remains in Me and I in him, he will bear much fruit; apart from Me you can do nothing,' we ask You to prune the branches of the vine. It is only through pruning that new life will come.

Often during prayers I sneaked a peek out of the corner of my eye. Sister Kathy was fifty-something. I guess she was still going through the change of life as her cheeks and neck glowed red and splotchy. The cross pinned to the collar of her crisp white blouse sparkled in the candlelight. She wore sensible walking shoes, a pleated skirt to below the knee, a woollen cardigan: very practical, non-fuss attire.

Jesus, without You we can do nothing. Abide in us so we can abide in You.

Sister Christine's voice was sweet and gentle. She looked a lot older than the others. Her white face, dark eyes and grey hair were encircled by a neat blue veil to her shoulders and a blue dress covered the rest of her pear-shaped figure. She wore a crucifix around her neck and carried Rosary beads in her pocket. She was the only member of the community who had opted to wear a modern version of the traditional religious habit. She was quiet, dignified and gracious; her prayer precise and succinct.

We thank You for the nourishment You give us in the Bread and Wine of Holy Communion.

We thank You for the Breath of Your Holy Spirit in our lives.

We thank You for the beautiful symbol of the vine.

You, the true vine; we, the branches, grafted into Your Body.

May we be effective in the regeneration of the lives of others, through our close communion with You.

Sister Maggie was modern and articulate. She was the principal of the college and carried most of the responsibility.

As You prune away the branches, Lord, heal the wounds of our hearts. As Sisters of the Sacred Heart of Jesus, make us one with You.

Sister Eleanor's voice barely touched the silence – she was lost in contemplation. Dressed in a blue and white knitted twin-set with matching navy blue skirt, bulletproof stockings and flat brown lace-up shoes, she seemed very old-fashioned. But her words were beautiful and I listened intently, eyes wide open.

I often watched the nuns during community prayer. Never once did I ever find one of them looking around the room, watching me.

Finally, Sister Kathy blew out the candle – the signal that prayers were finished for another night. I hadn't said a word to God or a word out loud. I couldn't quieten my thoughts, or find any words to express myself. My prayers had always been recited from a prayer book or learnt off by heart. I didn't feel very spontaneous, although I hoped I would, given a bit more time, as I developed a sense of belonging, a sense of community.

My mind was bombarded with images from my day at school. There was so much raw emotion, so many students who desperately needed understanding, sympathy, kindness and tolerance. I didn't know how to bring anything of that into night-time prayers; although I couldn't stop feeling like I was the one in the real world where it mattered, sharing God's love with those in need, and being relevant. If that was a proud thought, it was one I might have to confess.

After prayers Sister Maggie sometimes wanted to talk about the problems of her day. She talked quietly to Sister Eleanor. Was I supposed to listen or was it confidential? I didn't know, as nobody said anything, and nobody included me in conversation.

Invariably Sister Christine left the lounge first and I followed her out. I had problems of my own. Sister Maggie was responsible for a hundred college students whereas I was teaching six hundred students each week.

As the days turned to weeks, I realised I was still living with strangers whose focus was their relationship with an invisible being, namely God. I was young and didn't know how to connect with them. Each night, during dinner, the television filled the room, and prayers – a time of peaceful meditation and sharing – became a time of muddled reflection for me.

Also, I was living on the fringe of their world – new and unknown – and not yet allowed in. So I too began to live in my own world. I learned to relax, to be comfortable in the isolation. I hoped that somehow, someday, God might close the gap between us.

I'd left behind everything I ever knew when I joined their community. On that first weekend, Sister Eleanor had told me I wasn't allowed to visit my family or have them visit me. And I didn't even get a chance to talk to Father McSweeney in confession because the parish was too far away and I didn't have a car. So I found myself in an odd space where no one at school knew that I lived in a community of nuns, and no one in the community had any idea about my day at school. In fact, my day at school wasn't important to them. Their focus was on *their* schools and educational institutions that had become burdensome for them. The future of their institutions was uncertain because of the huge decrease in new candidates entering their Order. I understood that one day they would be *my* schools and educational institutions. However, I missed not having someone with whom I could discuss my day; to pick over the pieces, the squabbles and skirmishes and tiny successes.

This sense of isolation was heightened by an incident that occurred not long after I arrived. Sister Eleanor had informed me that I was to have a session of spiritual guidance with her each Sunday afternoon at four o'clock. However, after only the second session, she cancelled any further meetings.

"You don't have a whole lot of questions for me, Maria, so don't bother turning up next week," she said.

I hid my surprise.

"If you have any questions, at any time, I'm right here in my room. My door is always closed but just knock. Okay?"

What was I meant to make of that? It was confusing. This had been my opportunity to get to know someone in the community, one on one. So what had gone wrong? Was I too quiet? Did she think I was sullen or difficult? Or what?

In the first meeting she had opened the door to her room and invited me in. The window sill was cluttered with knick-knacks, the shelves jammed with books, the radiator draped in damp washing.

"Take a seat," she said, pointing to the only chair in the room. She seemed oblivious to the pantyhose hanging over the armrest.

I lowered myself into the seat and watched as she settled on the bed, surrounded by piles of unfolded washing.

"Now, what would you like to talk about?"

The size and scope of the question was mindboggling. I was bursting with details about my life at school: the bravery of one boy who had to cope with having a metal arm and hand, the kindness of another, who had defended me from the worst bullies in his class despite his own challenges of coping with dwarfism. But I knew these things weren't of any consequence to Sister Eleanor.

"I'm not sure."

An hour later I left, feeling less pessimistic. She had read from the Bible, shared a prayer, a thought or two, and so had I. It was a start.

The next week the room was still messy, the conversation less forced. An hour later I stepped into the corridor feeling lighter. Then she dropped the bombshell.

"Don't bother turning up next week."

Had she sensed my uneasiness? What questions should I have asked? I'd never shared anything about my spiritual life before. What did a spiritual life consist of, anyway? I didn't know. This was my opportunity to learn. All I needed was a little coaxing, a little time.

At school I coaxed and encouraged all day every day, like every other keen teacher – complimenting, smiling, pacifying, coercing, cajoling, questioning, teasing, joking, stimulating, challenging, and confirming. It wasn't that difficult.

I turned and walked along the corridor as Sister Eleanor closed her bedroom door, shutting me out.

I went to my room, since there was nowhere else to go, and sat at the desk, picked up the guitar and strummed a few chords. I missed my family, missed having someone to talk to. The student boarders were too young, their conversations about boyfriends and parties inappropriate for a budding nun, or so I thought.

I never returned to Sister Eleanor's room, and she never said a word about it. Every night at dinner I expected her to say something, to give me a little reassurance, but she never did.

Chapter 6
Bully in the Classroom

By the end of the first term I was used to herding students in and out of my room, day after day. I knew the names of my six hundred students: eighteen classes each week of Year 9 and 10 students. I was even starting to feel good about myself.

So, when the principal, Mr McCarthy, marched into the classroom one day unannounced, he caught me by surprise. Why was he visiting me? I hadn't done anything wrong.

He was a powerfully built man with huge shoulders and a beer gut hanging over his leather belt. Everyone was scared of him – the cane was still used liberally to mete out punishment to the boys.

I wasn't intimidated by Mr McCarthy because Dad had been best mates with his younger brother throughout their boyhood years and beyond. In a funny kind of way, Mr McCarthy seemed like family to me, although I'm sure he was unaware of this. However, he did know that I was Eddie Hall's daughter. And Eddie Hall had had a reputation for being a scallywag when he was at school. In his final year, Dad had deliberately broken the rules by wearing a green suit and maroon hat instead of the compulsory school uniform. To avoid detection from the uniform enforcer, he would dash through the bushes rather than exit through the school gates. His friends were in awe of him – he never got caught – and his reputation remained intact. But that was back in 1931.

So, who did Mr McCarthy see as he fixed his icy blue eyes on me?

"Maria, you were present at the staff meeting when the notes were handed out about the preparation of exam papers."

"Yes, that's right," I nodded.

All the windows in the music room opened out to the quadrangle where the whole school was waiting in bus lines. We had an audience.

"You know that there's a strict procedure that must be followed to the letter. The timetable set out in the notes must be adhered to. The office staff are absolutely magnificent but they cannot work miracles."

Miracles? That was a curious choice of words.

"There are fifteen hundred students in this school," he continued. "Every student is sitting at least five subjects. Do you have any idea how many exam papers that is?" Without pausing for a reply, he roared in fury, "Your exam papers were meant to be in the office last Friday for typing, printing and stapling. Bringing them in late is going to put everyone under huge pressure. I cannot stand for this! This behaviour of yours is totally unacceptable."

Beads of perspiration were popping out of the leathery skin on his forehead. Not good!

"You are meant to be behaving like a professional teacher. You, and you alone, are letting down the entire school. So what are you going to do about it?"

God almighty! The man was ready to explode. He was going to have a heart attack and I'd be blamed! The audience outside would make sure of that.

Steel your nerves. Look gently but steadily into his eyes. He's your dad's best mate's older brother.

"Your instructions re the exam papers state that if we do not have the exam questions into the office by said date, then we are personally responsible for the printing and stapling of them ourselves. I'm quite happy to prepare the exam papers myself. I know how to use the banda machine. I use it all the time. I've nearly written all the exam questions. However, I need a bit more inspiration to create a few more exciting questions."

He looked at me in shock.

"There's really nothing for you to worry about, Mr McCarthy."

That wasn't what he expected to hear. I glanced outside at the hundreds of students queuing in bus lines. He'd timed his performance perfectly. Little wonder everyone was scared of him. The kids were going to give me hell the next time they saw me.

"But you have so many students, Maria. That's a lot of work," he said sternly.

I reminded myself that I was Eddie and Pat Hall's daughter. I was capable, creative and strong. I had one of the worst timetables in the entire school: nine classes of Year 9 students and nine classes of Year 10 students every week. On average thirty to thirty-five students per class. All classes were streamed. Top streams had one period of music per week. Bottom streams had two periods per week. And some of the students in the bottom streams were brain-dead while others were psychos. There was no chance of any student, no matter how gifted, continuing with their music studies. From the students' point of view music was a fun subject, a time to muck around, to drum on the desk and make a racket.

However, the students liked me and I liked them. I had the best classroom in the school. A room with a view, and not just any view: I had a sea view of the Manukau Harbour. I could transport myself out of the classroom and into a boat any time I liked.

Mr McCarthy knew I was a first-year teacher, and learning to be a teacher without any support from anyone. He knew it was just me and the kids. I was the music department, the Head of Department with all the responsibility but without the fancy salary – in fact, without any salary at all. My salary was directly credited into the bank account of the Sacred Heart Order on Sister Amy's instruction.

As he strode out of the classroom I realised I'd learnt something from my students. I'd learnt how to stand up to a bully. I'd never done that before. Inside, I was trembling.

Over the next few nights I stayed up late, teasing out ideas. I needed two exam papers – one for each level. Two groups of three hundred students were due to sit in the school hall for a two-hour music exam, balancing pen and paper on their knees, and I wanted to design exams that would keep them interested and busy. With other teachers present, maintaining discipline and strict exam protocol, I had a captive audience.

Every spare moment at school was spent in the teachers' work room, printing and stapling thousands of pages of neatly handwritten questions into booklets. Was it really worth the extra effort?

A week later three hundred students, many laughing and joking, straggled out of the school hall after the exam.

"Good one, eh Miss." They gave me 'the eyes', that knowing look of approval as they raised their eyebrows in acknowledgment.

Even the ten teachers on exam duty in the hall appeared relaxed and happy as they chatted together.

"Did you see those kids in there? I've never seen them concentrating so hard, have you?" someone said.

"You're right. They didn't work like that in the maths exam this morning."

The maths teacher didn't sound very impressed.

The office staff had gathered at the back of the hall. The music for the exam, including themes from *The Muppets* and *Hawaii Five-O*, had been played through the sound system and filtered through to the school office. The office staff were giggling. Even the 'battleaxe' was grinning.

I congratulated myself that I'd survived the first term at school. Hopefully, I'd survive the next two terms, and then the year would be over.

Chapter 7
A Testing Time

During the May holidays all the nuns of the Sacred Heart Order in Auckland made the five-hundred kilometre journey to the capital city, Wellington, for a week of meetings at their sister school, Erskine College in Island Bay. The architecture of the college was impressive: exquisite French Gothic.

This was my first experience of living in a big community of nuns. Dear old nuns patted my hands with affection as we chatted and queued for meals, meetings and chapel. They didn't remember me, the girl with freckles and long ringlets whom they had taught. However, I remembered them and that's all that mattered to me. I had been a keen student but not a top student, elected again and again as a sports captain without ever having been in a sports team. Saturday morning sports clashed with Mass, music lessons and boating in my family.

We quickly filled in the roster of chores. This big family of nuns had to be fed. Someone asked me to play the guitar and lead the singing during Mass and community prayers every day. It was good to be acknowledged, to be allowed to contribute, and I wanted the experience to last the rest of the year. In comparison with my dreary life at Loreto Hall I was in heaven.

I felt so elated that each night I sneaked back into the chapel after everyone had gone to bed. I stayed there for hours on my own, praying and singing and making a big noise.

Every morning at breakfast I expected a comment from somebody; a pithy aside, a snide remark, a strong rebuke. But no one said a word. Obviously the building was solid, the soundproofing superb, and no one had heard me.

Although the week in Wellington was over far too soon, the experience lifted my spirits and I returned to Auckland, to the daily routine, feeling more confident.

During the second term at school, I contracted a bad dose of tonsillitis and went home to my parents to recuperate. It was good to be home and I realised how much I'd missed everyone. Mother was concerned I was sick and insisted that she take me to the doctor who questioned my suitability for teaching. Was I strong enough? Did I have enough stamina? Was I too sensitive?

Over the next few days, as my throat improved, I started to talk about my life at Loreto Hall for the first time, as up until this point all conversations had been internalised. Mother voiced her concerns about me not seeing anyone until six o'clock each night. Dad listened quietly. I reminded myself that my students provided plenty of opportunity for social interaction, and that my life at Loreto Hall provided time for contemplation, self-examination and spiritual growth. I had to toughen up and be more grateful. I only had to survive the year. Then I would move onto the next stage. Then everything would be better.

A week later I returned to Loreto Hall, but nothing changed.

The second term, a long winter's term, finally came to an end and the August holidays commenced. Instead of going home for a break, I spent time at Baradene College, caring for the elderly nuns in the infirmary.

Inspectors arrived at school during the final term. Fortunately, the principal approved of my request to be critiqued by the Inspectors and, therefore, be eligible for a Teacher's Certificate in this, my first year of teaching. Normally two years were required to qualify.

I told the students the Inspectors were checking on them, and that there would be serious consequences if they misbehaved. The threat worked, everyone behaved, and I received glowing comments from the Music Inspector who recommended that I receive the very much sought after Teacher's Certificate.

That one week of teaching was so enjoyable that, for a brief moment, I questioned my reasons for leaving. However, outside the school gates I knew I had another life, another focus, a holy purpose. I resigned as planned, a few weeks later.

The year had been difficult. I'd learnt that teaching in a co-educational state school, with no support from anyone, was not for cowards. Many students had fought me every day, never flinching in their resolve to win, to confront, to complain, to insult. However, now that the year was over, they decided it was time to be nice, to say thanks, and to give me presents. I marvelled at their cheek. But they made me feel special, something quite new for me, and it was great. I had to admit that I felt more connected to the students at Onehunga High School than to the small community of nuns at Loreto Hall.

At the end of year prize-giving ceremony, the school orchestra – under my baton – played 'Feelings' by Morris Albert and 'Sailing' by Rod Stewart. Two Year 11 girls who played the clarinet had chosen the music, which I orchestrated for them. The audience of two thousand responded with delight, the applause lasting far too long. The students in the orchestra had gone from being geeks to pop stars in the space of a few bars of music. The principal announced that he wished I wasn't leaving.

The following day, with mixed emotions, I tidied shelves, counted books, checked musical instruments, and updated the inventory. Then I returned the classroom keys to the school office for the very last time.

Back at Loreto Hall, student boarders were spring-cleaning their rooms and scrubbing wooden floors in the classrooms. I thought the nuns would give me something to do, too, so I was surprised when Sister Eleanor told me I could go home for Christmas. If I liked, I could leave the next day.

The television prevented any meaningful conversation over dinner that final night. No one facilitated any discussion about my initiation year at Loreto Hall. Not one word was said, not even in prayer; not even a word from Sister Eleanor. But she hadn't said much all year, not since she told me not to bother turning up to her room for the compulsory weekly session of spiritual guidance. I was the only one who wasn't astounded when she left the Order a few months later. To everyone else, she had been the epitome of dedication and devotion.

My inability to build any real rapport with them and their lack of interest or insight into how to connect with me, combined with feelings of exclusion from college life, had effectively silenced me. Even on that final night, I was unable to initiate any discussion with them or share my thoughts in vocal prayer.

All the nuns had friends and confidantes within the Order and among the college staff, women they had known most of their lives. They were part of a well-functioning social network of contacts built up over many years. I, on the other hand, was completely disconnected from my network of friends and family. In fact, I was banned from speaking to the latter. This was deliberate and designed to test me; to test the strength of my relationship with God. I had hoped I was strong enough, my love pure enough, generous enough. My life at Loreto Hall had been intended to provide me with time and opportunity for meditation and soul-searching. Isolation, solitude, quiet – essential requirements. No one, myself included, thought that this level of isolation might be unhealthy.

All my socialising had taken place at school among teenagers who challenged me in every possible way; teenagers who knew nothing about God. I pondered the significance of that. Did it matter?

Word had arrived from the Provincial Superior in Australia that I had been accepted for the next stage, and I accepted the invitation without any hesitation. I was focused on the concept of religious vocation as a calling from God and I was committed to that ideal. I was keen to leave behind the life at Loreto Hall – with its elusive questions, never uttered.

The next stage of training consisted of two years of study at the 'formation house' in Melbourne, Australia, where I would live in another convent of the Sacred Heart Order. I looked forward to living in a bigger community of nuns, some of whom were my age. I hoped to make some friends, and to reconnect with Sister Amy who was the Superior there. On three occasions, in preparation for my entering the Order the previous year, Amy had interviewed me at Baradene College when she was visiting from Australia. She had recommended some books, shared stories about her early years in the Order, and her overseas travel visiting other Sacred Heart communities. The conversations had been stimulating and I was hoping to pick up where we left off.

After spending Christmas at home with my parents, I packed a suitcase once again, and set off on the next stage of my journey.

Chapter 8
Life in the Oasis

In February 1977, after boarding a plane for Melbourne and crossing the vast ocean of the Tasman Sea for the first time in my life, I arrived at Tullamarine Airport where seven nuns were waiting to meet me. From a distance they looked like ordinary women dressed conservatively in trousers, skirts and blouses. As I got closer, small silver and gold crosses pinned to their collars sparkled in the bright light. And, on further scrutiny, I noted their fresh complexions with no makeup, no lipstick or fancy hairdos, identifying them as somewhat different from other women at the airport. They looked healthy and well-fed, with an aura of goodness and virtue.

We clambered into a waiting van and drove away from the airport, heading towards Camberwell in the eastern suburbs, and the formation house called Kadesh. The drive was a chance for a quick exchange of details and I listened carefully, putting faces to names I had heard mentioned the previous year.

"Maria, do you know anyone in our community?" someone asked.

"Only Amy," I said.

"Who do you think I am?" came the quick retort.

"I have no idea."

"I'm Amy," she said.

I looked, in disbelief, at the woman sitting opposite me. Nothing about the physical appearance of this Amy seemed familiar to me. This Amy was much thinner, with recently-cropped short hair and finely-plucked eyebrows. Away from Baradene College, it seemed I didn't know Amy at all.

There was a pause as everyone giggled, except me.

"Do you know the history behind the word 'Kadesh'?" Amy asked.

"No, I don't," I said politely.

"Kadesh means 'consecrated' or 'holy'."

I nodded an acknowledgment.

"During the forty years that Moses and the Israelites wandered in the desert after their escape from Egypt, they used the oasis of Kadesh as an important base camp."

Amy continued talking about Moses as we zigzagged our way along the highway. I gazed out the window at the changing scenery, noting the makes and models of passing cars, all quite different from vehicles in New Zealand.

From time to time I glanced across at her. I still couldn't find anything that was familiar. Even her mood seemed different.

"I wonder what Kadesh will mean for you, Maria," she said. "And if it will be your spiritual oasis as it was for Moses and the Israelites."

I wondered too. I knew I mustn't repeat the mistakes of the previous year. And, of equal importance and curiosity to me, was Amy's own apparent transformation since last we met.

Kadesh, a stately Victorian two-storey house, was shielded from the main road by a high hedge.

As we climbed out of the van, the urban soundscape exploded in the scorching heat of a summer's day – cicadas chirping, birds twittering, trams clanging, brakes screeching.

The house was spacious. The presence of two staircases, back to back, hinted that servants had been part of the original household a century earlier. My upstairs bedroom was sparsely furnished. Yet another lumpy mattress on the bed reminded me of the vow of poverty.

We prayed together in the lounge after dinner and washing-up that first night. The room was large and comfortable, its dark green wallpaper heavily embossed, bordered by wide scotias, architraves and skirtings painted white. A handsome fireplace and mantelpiece dominated one wall. Cosy sofas and armchairs were positioned tastefully around the television. Floor-to-ceiling shelves were stacked with hundreds of books.

I wasn't the only newcomer to the community as two other nuns, older than me, had flown into Melbourne earlier in the week. They were also settling in and assessing their new surroundings.

There were nine of us at Kadesh: four Australians and three New Zealanders, ranging in age from mid-thirties to late-fifties, plus Donna and me, aged twenty-five and twenty-three. She and I were the only two in training. All the nuns were educators – strong-minded and decisive – except for the one who was a librarian.

This was meant to be a full-time study year for me. I was attending lectures at Yarra Theological College and I set my mind to the first essay: the meaning of Faith in St Paul's Letters to the Romans. I'd always enjoyed study and expected that this latest experience would be stimulating. Previously I'd exceeded my lecturers' expectations at university as I devoured dozens of obscure books on music history and classical composers. Now I was studying something new, about my favourite person, Jesus.

At home at Kadesh, I settled in, quietly observing the personality and spirituality of each member of the community. I watched as petty jealousy and rivalry surfaced, laying bare the vulnerability and humanity of each of them. Some of them had known one another from their first day at school aged five. After all the squabbling in my own classroom the previous year, I was relieved these latest battles weren't mine to resolve.

The older nuns had witnessed big changes in the Order during the previous ten years. The original Book of Rules, that had governed their lives from the moment they had entered the Order, had been replaced by a new book, written in response to the guidelines laid down by Vatican Council II. This newly-updated book used modern language and ideas to explain the spirituality, mission and organisation of the Sacred Heart Order, and those ideas were still being tested and interpreted.

Under the new rules, a change of Superior took place in all convents every year, with each nun casting her vote. But not at Kadesh because Amy refused to allow an election. She stated her case: it was only logical that she retain her position as Superior, at the top of the pyramid, because she was the Novice Mistress and responsible for the formation of new nuns. She said she had the support of the Provincial Superior of Australasia. Several nuns expressed their discontent, one vehemently, hoping for a shift in power, but to no avail. Amy was immovable.

When I wasn't sitting on a wooden seat in a lecture room at Yarra Theological College, I had lectures at home with Amy, and Donna who was a year ahead of me. The day commenced with the private recitation of the Daily Office in the chapel – a selection of prayers, readings and reflections for each day of the year. Then we went to Mass at the local church of Our Lady of Victories, named after the battle between Christian and Turkish forces in the Gulf of Lepanto in 1571. The church was Byzantine/Romanesque in style, with a stone exterior and dozens of magnificent stained glass windows. Breakfast followed, then class, in-house.

While Amy lectured, we listened in silence, seated on beanbags in her room. I was quickly bored but Donna seemed content to simply listen. We were studying the prophets of the Old Testament and the subject material was familiar to me. Amy knew this as, on her recommendation, I had spent the year prior to Loreto Hall studying at a Catholic theological college.

I waited for an opportunity to ask a question, offer a comment or shift the focus just a little. I was being subtle, and respectful. I saw a real opportunity to converse on a deeper spiritual level and I hoped that Amy was smart enough to make some changes. I didn't want a repetition of the previous year – Maria being mute and feeling isolated – so I waited patiently, picking my moments carefully.

After class I headed to my room to read for the essay on Faith. My lecturer, Father Jerome Crowe, was an internationally-acclaimed scripture scholar and author, and I was lucky to be in his class. He was about fifty years old, with white hair, receding hairline, and glasses. He delivered an even drier monologue than Amy but there was definitely no opportunity to interrupt him, and no one dared. The only distraction during class came from the raucous squawking and happy chatter of kookaburras and magpies, perching in huge trees in the park-like grounds.

The college was purpose-built with lecture rooms, sweeping corridors and covered walkways. Groups of nuns from various Religious Orders mingled with laypeople and crowds of Catholic seminarians, training for the priesthood. I'd never seen so many handsome Catholic men in my whole life. It wasn't long before I heard who were the scoundrels and who the saints. And who got drunk on Saturday night.

Lectures finished at midday and everyone climbed into cars and vans and returned to their seminaries and convents. From time to time, I caught a ride from one of the priests who dropped me close to a tram stop. Riding on the tram was one of the few opportunities I had to be in the secular world, away from Catholic influence.

Each afternoon, hidden in my bedroom, I had plenty of time to think. My change of role from teacher to student required some adjustment and it wasn't easy for me. I missed teaching; the kids, the energy, the interaction and noise of the classroom. I forced myself to recall all the worst aspects: the snotty noses, the infected earlobes, the skin rashes. I could smell the bad body odour and greasy hair. It helped a bit.

I buried myself in books, but inside I was fidgety like never before. I was meant to be focused on a spiritual goal, of committing my life to God in the service of the Church. This was my one ambition, my big dream. It was meant to fill me with joy and happiness. But, something was wrong.

I was obliged to follow the path laid down for me. Obedience was required, lectures unavoidable. I had to submit, to put self aside. I chided myself for being disgruntled. After all, what did I know? Who did I think I was? Where was my humility?

In an effort to find a little personal happiness, I decided to explore a creative approach to the essay writing rather than an academic one. So I stopped reading and started writing. If I could engage heart and soul, not just intellect, I hoped my mood might change. Eventually, I decided to write a poem and I hoped the lecturer, Father Jerome Crowe, would appreciate the effort.

One afternoon when I arrived home from college, Father Jim, the psychologist, was standing in the lounge talking to the other nuns.

"Jim, this is Maria, our newest baby nun," Barbara said as I entered the room.

Baby nun... I balked at the words.

"She's a Kiwi, our latest candidate from New Zealand," Barbara continued.

"We've already met, Maria and I," he said, giving me a smile. "At Baradene College. Nice to see you again, Maria."

"Hello, Jim."

Everyone else was shaking hands with him so I stepped forward to do the same. But instead of shaking hands with me, he took my right hand in his left, so that he and I were holding hands.

What was he thinking? What were the nuns thinking? I felt awkward, stuck in the middle of the circle – all eyes on me. I relaxed my fingers, willing him to let go, but he held on. I shuffled my feet, trying to get out of the centre of the circle. I glanced from face to face; some nuns were looking embarrassed.

Perhaps he saw himself as a modern day Jesus figure. But it didn't feel right to me even though I knew I shouldn't question his integrity. Five minutes of handholding seemed interminable. He really was making a statement. But what was I meant to infer from the handholding?

As soon as he let go, I headed to the kitchen and made a cup of coffee. Ten minutes later he left and I resurfaced. I went to my room to work on the poem. I had found a way to make exegesis or hermeneutics – the critical explanation or interpretation of scripture – enjoyable.

A couple of weeks later, I handed in the assignment, and then waited. I was pleased with the final version and thought I might share the four-page poem with the nuns during evening prayer. One of the nuns had been my English teacher in Year 10 and I was sure she would appreciate it.

Unfortunately, Father Jerome Crowe wasn't impressed, and he gave me a big fat F for fail. But I didn't care; actually, I was slightly amused. The experience had been meaningful and that was what mattered to me.

I mentioned to some of the nuns at Kadesh that I'd failed my first assignment.

"I'd be interested in reading it, Maria," my ex-English teacher said. "On what grounds did the lecturer fail you?"

"He couldn't relate to the use of the impersonal pronoun 'it' in place of the word 'faith', or the format of a poem over an essay."

"I'd still like to read it," she said.

Amy said, "You should be taking advantage of your educational opportunities, not squandering them."

That sounded like a putdown.

"All this study could go towards a Bachelor of Theology," she continued. "It could be useful in the future."

No more silent rebellion, I told myself. My future in the Order was unknown as yet, but others, in particular Amy, would have a say. I needed to listen, and be open to the Holy Spirit working through her, even if what was asked of me was contrary to my own ideas.

Chapter 9
Mary's Submission

"Donna!" I called from the bottom of the staircase. "It's time for class."

There was no reply. I called again. Louder. Still no reply. I waited downstairs, wondering where she was.

Amy didn't tolerate tardiness and Donna was usually punctual, keen to please. And keen to set a good example for me, the youngest in the community.

Amy appeared from the kitchen, head held high, and walked along the hallway towards her bedroom where the three of us were to have class. She paused at the doorway and turned to face me.

"Maria, Donna's having class on her own from now on." Her tone was serious.

"Ah… What do you mean?" I started frowning.

"Donna's having class on her own from now on," she repeated. "Come in and sit down and we'll pray about it."

Confused, I followed her into her room. She closed the door. I stayed standing, mouth half-open.

"Sit down," she said.

A crucifix hung above the bed, catching the morning light. An exquisite icon of the Madonna, Our Lady of Perpetual Help, balanced on the wooden desk. I slumped into a beanbag, adjusting my long skirt around my ankles. Amy sat down, too.

"You see, Maria, Donna feels intimidated by you. She's not confident, academically, so I'm giving her classes on her own from now on."

Amy's voice was flat. I was flabbergasted. What could I say? It didn't make sense. But I couldn't contradict the Superior. She wasn't asking for my opinion anyway.

She lit a candle, placed it on the floor between us, and closed her eyes. As she prayed aloud I only half listened. I was lost in my own thoughts. Why hadn't I been informed earlier? Why hadn't I been involved in the process? How long had these discussions been going on? I was no academic, no big brain. I'd failed my first assignment at college, remember? How could she be intimidated by me? It seemed ridiculous.

It upset me that she had only considered Donna's feelings. As the youngest in the community, couldn't I expect a little consideration too?

Amy's prayer oozed sweetness about trusting God. About being open, letting God in, and waiting for God. About being humble, like Mary, the mother of God.

But why was I the only one who had to practice those beautiful virtues? Was there no place for compromise? Negotiation? Simple honest conversation?

When Amy finished her prayer she opened her exercise book to begin the class. I glanced at the pages. The handwriting was neat. She started to read from her lecture notes, slowly and deliberately, like she always did.

I waited to see how things might change to accommodate the new arrangement. But nothing changed. Amy didn't try to engage me in discussion, even though Donna wasn't present. I guessed that when I was attempting to participate in the class I was, in fact, interrupting her. And she didn't want to be interrupted by me. I was meant to be quiet and listen. Nothing more.

I was meant to submit like Mary, Jesus' mother. Mary submitted to God, and God blessed her by sending the Holy Spirit and showering her with grace. She conceived Jesus, the Son of God, our Saviour and Redeemer. Amy constantly reminded me that Mary was our role model of submission to the will of God.

After that day Donna kept a low profile when in the house. She mostly hid in her room where she studied alone. Her transistor radio, tuned to Talkback, filled the void.

News of the fallout quickly filtered through the community. Everyone, almost without exception, quietly voiced their disapproval to me of the new arrangement. It seemed Amy wasn't popular with everyone but she was the Superior. She was the Novice Mistress and I was the novice, not that that old-fashioned language was used anymore. In fact, those words had been thrown out with the old Book of Rules and no new words had been invented; at least not then. But in religious communities as old as ours, and as old as the Catholic Church itself, no matter how many rules changed, titles and terminology stuck, loaded with centuries of symbolism and meaning.

As Melbourne's long summer days came to an end, I took extra study breaks in the afternoon. I headed to the chapel, which was modern and unconventional. It was a big bright room at the front of the house dominated by three powerful religious symbols. A fishing net, hanging across the ceiling, reminded me that Jesus' first apostles were fishermen. A cross, made of two rough-sawn pieces of timber, represented the depth of God's love. A large rock in the centre of the room represented the Magisterium of the Church, the authority of Saint Peter, the first Pope.

On top of the rock sat a gold box. Inside the box was a small white Host: the Body of Christ – a reminder of Jesus' promise to be with us always. A few cushions lay scattered on the carpeted floor.

A cane blind acted as a partition at the entrance to the chapel. I liked to sit behind the blind, hidden from view, guitar on lap, waiting. Waiting like Mary, Jesus' mother, for the Holy Spirit to descend on me, like Amy had instructed. Waiting for peace and joy to fill my heart.

I flicked through the Bible, searching for inspiration in The Psalms. I strummed a twelve-string guitar, and hummed softly. I hoped I wasn't disturbing anyone, and I wished I had a soundproof room so I could make as much noise as I liked. Great depths of emotion were locked up inside me – ambiguity, frustration, annoyance and desperation – smothered in layers of faith, hope and love.

One night I shared one of my songs with the nuns during evening prayer. It was a positive experience. I was laying bare my soul, sharing with the community, like I was supposed to. Amy and Donna weren't present because they were out of town for the week and, in their absence, I felt more relaxed.

After prayers the candle was blown out and lights switched on. Everyone knew that Bernadette wanted to watch television. She always did, every night, on her own.

"What did you mean by those lyrics, Maria? Can I have a look at them?" Josie asked. She was a music teacher, like me. "Have you got them written down?"

It was a perfect opportunity to engage me in some conversation. Me, Maria, who hardly ever spoke.

"Lyrics don't need to be analysed," Janet, the English teacher, chipped in. She sounded cross. "They just 'are'. Let them be."

Josie and I glanced at one another, then at Janet. Janet knew what she was talking about. The other nuns watched in silence. Bernadette was fiddling with the television remote. It was an awkward moment. It would have been nice to have had a conversation. They talked all day at school but I didn't have much opportunity to talk to anyone. I didn't even talk in class with Amy, anymore. She had managed to get her pupil to shut up and listen.

Janet stood up and left the room. Josie followed and so did I. We went to our rooms and closed our doors as required, effectively shutting everyone else out.

Chapter 10
Experimenting with Change

Josie sat down on a white-painted stool in the kitchen. She leant her elbows on the table – a big, green Formica table which filled the centre of the room. It was cluttered with pots and pans.

"What are you making tonight, Maria?" she asked.

"Beef lasagne," I said. It was Thursday, my night for cooking.

Josie sipped her coffee, her glasses steaming up. Her jet-black hair was now a bit messy after a long day at school. I glanced in her direction, mindful of the tiredness showing on her face.

"Let me move some of those things out of your way," I said, wiping my hands on my apron.

Earlier in the day I had visited the open-air food market in the centre of Camberwell, a few hundred metres down the road from Kadesh. I always enjoyed the experience: dozens of stalls piled high with exotic vegetables and fruits, spicy salamis, strings of sausages and smelly cheeses, showcasing little pockets of Europe. I felt transported by the spirited laughter and serious haggling. The intensity of the young with dark eyes and flawless skin. The fragility of the old, dressed in black, with wrinkles and white hair, the women rubbing shoulders with their men folk. The pungent smell of tobacco filling the air. The marketplace humming with Italians and Greeks and happy shoppers, and I was a part of it.

I stirred the salsa, simmering on the stove.

"You need more in your life, Maria," Josie said. "I could show you where to find the key for the organ loft at Our Lady of Victories. You could play the organ there anytime you like. It's a pipe organ."

I turned to face her. "Really? But I'm not an organist."

She lowered her voice, switching her gaze towards the half-open door. "You can play the piano, can't you?"

"Yes."

She leaned in, closer. Did she think someone was lurking out of sight in the corridor, eavesdropping? Did the community operate like that? There had certainly been lots of muttering on the stairs over the incident with Amy splitting up our class.

"I'll teach you how to do the fingering. It's easy once you know how." Her lips were mouthing the words but her focus was definitely on the corridor. "I've got lots of organ music in my room and I could lend you some, if you like."

I concentrated on the corridor – I couldn't hear any footsteps.

"That would be great. Thanks very much. I'd love to play the organ."

"The organ at Our Lady of Victories is magnificent. Undoubtedly one of the best in Australia."

She seemed to relax, now that I'd consented. We arranged to meet on the weekend as she gulped the rest of her coffee. Then she got up, placed her cup in the sink, and walked into the corridor. I was sure no one was out there. I took the salsa off the stove to cool, before laying out the lasagne.

Josie had concerns – about what, though? Amy seemed the only person in the community who could possibly object to Josie's suggestion. I suspected that Josie was reliving her own formation experience, of thirty years ago, and comparing it with mine. Or, perhaps, there was a history of disagreement between the two women. It seemed unlikely, though, because Josie was a sweet, genuine woman. It could be a long time before I had any further insight, if at all.

In comparison with my experience at Loreto Hall, my life now was so much better. Despite the internal frustrations, I was committed to the idea of a religious vocation. I was waiting for God to strengthen my spirit. To give me the grace to endure, to empty myself of all desire, and to obey – willingly, blindly. I was striving for perfection, moment by moment.

The kitchen had become my favourite place. It was a room where people were human and where I felt a sense of belonging. The nuns enjoyed their food and I enjoyed cooking for them, especially as they were so appreciative.

We ate dinner, Monday to Friday, in the formal dining room that was next to the kitchen. The décor in the dining room was elegant Queen Anne mahogany furniture, setting the tone for dinner. Conversation around the table was limited; everyone was too busy eating. And, unlike Saturday nights in the seminary, there was no alcohol on the table to loosen our tongues, not that I knew anything about alcohol.

On weekends the atmosphere at Kadesh was more relaxed as nuns strolled in and out of the kitchen, preparing their own meals according to their likes and dislikes. I was surprised to see that each nun still had personal preferences. I had imagined that after years in the Order they would be so detached from everything, including food, that they would eat anything. But I was wrong. I was comparing the apparent virtue of the nuns at Kadesh with the spirituality found in a book I was studying at college: *The Cloud of Unknowing*, a fourteenth-century treatise on mysticism.

During lunch Ruth cut her apple into perfectly equal slices, delicately placing each piece into her mouth with a fork. Amy lowered her eyes modestly, chewing with concentration. In between bites, Barbara sat perfectly still, hands clasped neatly on her lap, eyes focused straight ahead. It was easy to imagine someone counting, inaudibly, ready to give the signal for everyone to swallow in unison.

There were no elbows on the table, no eating with one's mouth full, no interrupting, no talking at once, and no raucous laughter. This family of nuns was used to a rule of silence, to a bell pealing, to a frilly white wimple around the face, shielding the eyes. This family of nuns was used to squashing their curiosity and controlling their runaway thoughts.

The severe black habit was gone, replaced by normal clothing. A superficial transformation, at least, had taken place. The real challenge needed to go deeper, into the head and heart. The instruction from Pope Paul VI in Rome was for authenticity and renewal. Throwing out the habit was the easy bit; being relevant and effective in a modern world was more demanding. For the first time in their lives their opinions mattered as they tried to discern the workings of the Holy Spirit; hence Josie felt entitled to talk to me – but still with some apprehension.

It was inevitable that there would be mistakes as they toyed with new ideas – ideas that were strange and unfamiliar to them – especially with no one except religious men and women to steer them on that path. My initiation year in Auckland and formation year in Melbourne were part of that experiment with change.

Amy's directives went so far as to suggest that I find a friendly young seminarian to have as a companion. Donna had such a friend and sometimes she went out on a lunch-date with him. However, since at that stage I didn't know any seminarians well enough to organise a lunch-date, I never went out socialising and that was fine by me.

Amy never gave me any advice as to the nature of the possible friendship I was meant to nurture with a seminarian of my choosing. I assume I was meant to know innately or magically. Presumably, she thought she was encouraging me to be a modern nun, and to be normal, to enjoy male companionship. But what was normal for a nun? The idea of a chaste, virginal budding nun having a deep, meaningful relationship with a chaste, virginal seminarian seemed very odd to me. The last thing I needed was a handsome man capturing my interest and exciting my passions. I had enough of a struggle with nocturnal libido every night in bed all on my own without any encouragement from a frustrated, young, would-be priest. Not that I had any language to describe those thoughts.

Chapter 11
At Bedtime

The life of a nun precluded any deliberate sexual gratification of any kind – both in thought and in deed. 'Sexual pleasure' and 'self-abuse' were other phrases I associated with that forbidden act, although I didn't understand exactly why it was considered abusive and sinful. It was merely an instinct, although infuriating, and one I neither wanted nor seemed able to control. Nevertheless, I was able to quieten my curiosity and trust God to enlighten me when He was ready. And, in the meantime, I battled on, conscious that any lapse from the path of abstinence and chastity had to be confessed as a sin.

The words, "Bless me, Father, for I have sinned. It is one week since my last confession," were easy enough to say. But the next sentence could be more tricky, depending on the nature of the sins I had committed.

"I accuse myself. I have been uncharitable in my thoughts, three times. And I have been proud on a number of occasions. I also need to confess sins against chastity, on two occasions."

At that point my cheeks burned with shame as I concentrated on the stillness behind the black curtain. I listened for the priest's response, hiding in the dark but unable to hide from my own conscience.

"Alone or with another?" The priest always sounded stern.

"Alone, Father," I would whisper.

Then I'd have some doubts. Should I have said something else? But what? Was I keeping something back? No, I had confessed. I had said enough. I needed to wait for him to respond.

Once, when I confessed at the local church of Our Lady of Victories, I was horrified when the priest asked, "Are you with the community of nuns up the road?"

Instant terror! He must have realised that I was at Mass that morning and had waited for confessions to commence.

"Yes, Father," I whispered.

"This is not acceptable. This must never happen again. Do you understand?" He sounded angry. "Have you taken vows?"

"No, Father."

"But you're hoping to?"

"Yes, Father."

"When?"

This priest was definitely too nosey. He wasn't supposed to be interrogating me.

"I have no idea. My Superior has never mentioned vows to me."

"You understand this must never happen again, don't you?"

I would never be able to look him in the eye again.

"Yes, Father."

"Is there anything else?"

I resolved this would be my last confession to him. Reprimanding me didn't help. I chided myself all the time. I begged God to help me but it seemed He was testing my patience. Maybe He was letting me fall in order to humble me. Maybe I really was too proud. *Serves me right*, I thought. But did God work like that? I didn't know.

"No, Father."

"Are you sure?"

"Yes, Father."

"For your penance you will pray three 'Hail Marys', meditating on the purity of the Blessed Virgin Mary and her total submission to the will of God."

"Yes, Father."

"Now, say a good Act of Contrition."

"Oh my God, I am heartily sorry for having offended thee. I detest my sins above every other evil because they offend thee my God, who in thy infinite goodness art so deserving of all my love. And I firmly resolve by the help of thy grace, never to offend thee again, to avoid the occasion of sin and to amend my life. Amen."

"Go in peace, my child, and sin no more."

I was so relieved when I left the confessional. I had a clean slate. God had forgiven me. I could make a new start. Mother's favourite saying came to mind: *The road to hell is paved with good intentions.* New Zealand seemed like a long way away. I knew I had to try harder.

This was my second year of training to become a nun and there were new challenges. Chastity was the ideal path, the pinnacle of virtue. I was striving to achieve total detachment from everything and everyone, to empty myself of any human desire, especially any sexual desire.

I had made some progress, though. No longer did I fantasize about any particularly gorgeous guy on my radar. But, despite this, my body had feelings of its own which operated independently of my will. It was those physical feelings I was hoping to eliminate.

Priests, brothers and nuns had been taking vows of chastity for centuries. If they could do it, so could I. Obviously I needed to have more faith in God and He would sustain me. He would work miracles. Jesus proved He was the Son of God by working miracles when He was on earth. Surely, He would work miracles for me.

At times brief flashes of anger dominated my senses – anger at God because He wasn't quenching the fire at night in my bed. It wasn't fair. He was allowing me to suffer and fall. I consoled myself with the image of Jesus falling under the weight of the cross, remembering the words from scripture: *The spirit is willing but the flesh is weak.*

Sitting on the floor in the chapel I poured out my heart in song. I longed to be transformed into something more spiritual and ascetic and, therefore, less carnal, less needy. Song-writing helped me analyse my thoughts and feelings, comforting me. Outside, oak trees were shedding their leaves. I was straining to shed my old self, too.

Autumn leaves paved the tree-lined streets of Camberwell, swirling into the driveway at Kadesh. Some leaves still retained their vibrant reds, oranges and yellows, bringing to mind warmer days. And, just like the leaves had found a new home, I had found a friend at college. Or rather, Father Jerome Crowe, the lecturer who'd failed my poem, had befriended me. Sometimes he gave me a lift home.

One day as I stepped out of his car I picked up a leaf from the driveway.

"That's for you," I laughed, handing it to him.

I'd caught him by surprise. He blushed but didn't take it.

"It's a present," I said, as I placed it on the dashboard for him to admire.

"Thank you," he said. "Will you be at college tomorrow?"

"Yep."

"And the nuns would like me to say Mass on Thursday, this week?"

"If that's convenient for you."

"In that case I'll be here on Thursday, at 5:30. I'll give you a ride home then, too, if you like. You can let me know tomorrow."

We hardly ever had Mass in the chapel. Half the nuns at Kadesh were from New Zealand and the other half weren't originally from Melbourne, so we didn't have many connections with local priests.

I closed the car door and waved good-bye. Father Jerome smiled back. My spirit was light and carefree as I tip-toed over the multi-coloured carpet of leaves which covered the white pebbled driveway. Every leaf was a work of art.

Father Jerome came to Kadesh for Mass that week as agreed. I laughed as I gave him a hug at the Sign of Peace before Holy Communion. He smiled and blushed. The other nuns looked on in surprise. They shook his hand, formally.

"Peace be with you, Father," they said.

Some of them hugged one another, others shook hands.

The friendship between Jerome and I had started in his study at college. He had invited me and another nun, Sister Joan, to have lunch with him each day. He was a pleasant host, comfortable in his own space. He and Sister Joan conversed easily as he boiled the kettle and made us cups of soup. She knew how priests and nuns behaved behind closed doors and I was learning. She looked like a nun, dressed in her blue and white habit. She was older than me, closer in age to Jerome.

I stared at the papers on his desk, trying to get some sense of who he was, hoping I didn't seem too nosey. I was a bit in awe of him, but as the weeks passed I became less tongue-tied. We were three unlikely friends, having lunch together; being human, being real, trying to bridge the gap in age, culture, and status.

A few months later I invited Jerome to visit us again. After Mass he stayed for dinner. The conversation around the table was thought-provoking and spiritual. Nine eager faces, hanging on every word, were turned to the top of the table where he sat. He was the shepherd of the flock, the spiritual leader, a scholar and an author – admired and revered. I felt pleased. I had managed to get one of the most respected priests in Australia to sit at our dinner table and everyone was participating.

Two bottles of wine shared between ten had loosened silent tongues and softened morose temperaments. Even the most timid soul seemed less reticent.

Over the next few months Jerome visited us several times. On his last visit, he found me in the kitchen with Amy. I was busy preparing a salad. He stood behind me, gently massaging the back of my neck in a gesture of warmth and familiarity. I glanced across at Amy, and blushed.

Chapter 12
Danger

Most of the nuns at Kadesh went walking each afternoon. No one ever invited me to join in and I didn't ask to be included. Some hinted they wanted to be alone. Others teamed up with a best friend. Extras were not welcome.

Since the weather was perfect – cold and crisp with clear blue skies – I decided to go walking, too, but alone. After sitting bolt upright at the organ of Our Lady of Victories for an hour or two each day, playing complex contrapuntal Bach Preludes, I needed to stretch my legs.

The first signs of spring growth had appeared. Buds and bulbs in carefully-manicured gardens were still wet with dew. The sweet scent of jonquils and freesias hung loosely in the air, embracing my silent soliloquy.

One day a bubbly young girl stopped to talk to me. Another time an elderly couple asked about life in the convent. They had recognised me from church.

Depending on my mood I walked in a new direction each day, either sticking to the main roads bustling with rush-hour traffic, or meandering down quiet residential streets. I kicked my way through piles of leaves snapping under my feet as my thoughts wandered aimlessly. Josie was right: I needed more in my life. And practising the organ each day was helping.

I peered through cracks in fences. Behind wrought-iron gates. Into darkened windows. Feeling inquisitive.

On one particular day, hearing footsteps behind me, I moved onto the grass verge to make room for someone else to pass.

"G'day, how are you?"

I turned to see a young man, smiling.

"Hi," I said.

We chatted for a while. He said his name was Carlos. He asked how old I was in a thick European accent. Then he asked how old I thought he was. A stupid question, I thought, turning to face him.

Fine lines around his dark eyes aged him. "Thirty," I replied.

"What? I'm not that old!"

I noted the wounded pride.

"I'm twenty-seven," he said.

I shrugged, willing him to move on.

The conversation continued aimlessly for a few more minutes.

"Would you like to have a coffee?" he finally asked.

I looked at my watch. It was 4:43 pm. There was plenty of time before dinner, but coffee with strangers wasn't on my to-do list.

He only wants to talk, I reminded myself. What was the point of me being a Christian if I refused to be kind to strangers?

As a teenager I had been so vivacious, the liveliest girl in the parish. But I had changed.

Living with nuns had turned my focus inwards, making me introverted.

"Okay," I sighed.

We turned to walk back to Burke Road. The shopping centre at Camberwell was nearby, and had a good choice of cafés.

Carlos was tall and handsome, with shiny black hair and long sideburns. Dressed in jeans, leather boots and a chunky cream polo neck jumper, I found myself noticing various details about him.

"I have a car," he said, pointing to an old blue Ford Falcon, parked some metres away.

At the time I thought it odd that his car was parked nearby. I was walking in my neighbourhood and I assumed he was, too. However, I had agreed to the coffee and didn't want to go back on my word, so I squashed any misgivings as I opened the car door.

Seconds later, my instincts kicked back in, reminding me to be cautious. We turned the corner and stopped at the next intersection, watching for a passing tram.

"I live near here," he said. "So why don't we have that cup of coffee at my place?"

I didn't want to be negative or suspicious. I didn't want to be a coward. This was an opportunity for me to be strong, to test my faith, my trust in God. So, I said a cautious "Yes."

He parked outside a brick and tile townhouse. Everything inside was surprisingly neat and tidy; the furniture modern, the colour scheme neutral. He put the kettle on to boil. A guitar was leaning against the fireplace. I picked it up. It needed tuning and the tone was terrible.

We sipped our coffees. I encouraged him to talk. His family was scattered all over Europe. He came to Australia because it was the land of opportunity. He was ambitious, but life was difficult. He complained that his poor language skills hindered his business opportunities.

He turned on the stereo. He liked The Eagles. I heard him singing along in the kitchen, and he had a pleasant voice. He was boiling the kettle again. We both liked our coffee black, with two sugars.

I tried to explain that I was a student of scripture and theology, and that I was an aspiring nun. But he didn't understand those words. And my long denim skirt and maroon needle cord jacket certainly didn't identify me as a religious woman.

An hour or more slipped by. He alluded to family problems in Europe: of running away at sixteen to avoid conscription in the army, and of boarding a plane for Australia because he had fallen out with his brothers. I listened, without prying. Then he asked if I would like to stay for dinner and I said I would. He could pick up a pizza in Camberwell. I liked that idea. I had started to relax. It felt so good to talk, to laugh; so very normal.

He left me in the apartment while he went to get the pizza. I sat on the sofa, noticing for the first time that all the walls were bare. There was nothing personal anywhere, except the cheap guitar. I rang the convent and said I'd been delayed, that I'd be home later.

When he returned, we sat on the floor and ate the pizza. He drank a glass of red wine but I didn't drink anything. Then he leant over and kissed me, unexpectedly. I wasn't meant to enjoy it but I did. He'd caught me off-guard.

He asked for my phone number and I gave it to him. I saw no problem with that. Amy was still encouraging me to find a friend – maybe Carlos would be that special friend. Maybe I'd even help him find Jesus, not that I knew anything about his religious beliefs.

Shortly before midnight Carlos took me back to the convent. As he drove off, a wave of emotion swept over me, drowning me in physical pain and a sense of separation and loss that I couldn't possibly understand. I hardly knew the man, having spent only a few hours in his company. But they were the happiest few hours I'd had since coming to Melbourne. I believed in love above everything else and there was so little love in my life, so little friendship.

Kadesh was in darkness, both outside doors locked. I didn't have a key to get in and I didn't want to disturb anyone so I sat outside on a ledge in the garage. After a few hours I started to shiver from the cold. By morning I was utterly exhausted; I hadn't slept all night.

At half past seven I found the back door unlocked and made my way inside. There was no one around. I climbed the stairs to my room, closing the door softly. I needed to sleep but I knew sleep would be impossible. Daylight streamed into my room through flimsy unlined curtains. I flopped onto the bed. It was going to be a very long day. Amy was out of town for the week, and no one else would be checking on me, so I was free to do whatever I liked.

A couple of doors opened and closed downstairs. Everyone was leaving for school. I decided to go to Mass and then study in my room, as usual.

When the nuns returned from school I casually mentioned I'd bumped into a friend rather than I'd made a new friend. I wasn't sure how to describe the events of the previous day but since no one seemed interested, I didn't volunteer any more information.

On Sunday afternoon Carlos and I met as planned. He said he was thinking of buying a house and suggested we drive to a new housing subdivision. I'd grown up with parents whose favourite past-time was looking at real estate so I talked confidently about house prices in New Zealand. However, when we got to the subdivision Carlos changed his mind and drove past the open home sign. He said he'd look at it another day, on his own.

He turned onto the Nepean Highway and drove out of the city. It was a glorious spring day, perfect for a drive in the countryside. He acted like a tour guide. Eventually, he veered off the highway and the landscape changed from lanky gum trees to dense bush.

He turned down a dirt road and pulled over. The place was deserted: no people, no houses, no cars. He switched off the ignition.

He didn't say a word as he reached across and lowered the back of my seat. Then he climbed on top of me and unzipped his trousers before sliding his hand up my skirt. I didn't know what to think or what to do. He tugged at my pantyhose and pulled them down. I was scared.

Finally I found my voice. "I've got my period," I whispered.

I wanted him to stop but he ignored me and kept tugging.

"I've got my period," I repeated, this time, louder. He pulled my pants down as he looked at the blood on my sanitary pad. What kind of man did a thing like that? It was unnerving. I was in real trouble and I knew it. Any thought I had that Carlos was a decent guy vanished in horror.

His body pinned me down as he prised my legs apart with his knees. I squirmed in the seat as he forced himself inside me. Every muscle in my body locked tight as I strained to protect myself. He pushed and thrust, breathing deeply, developing a rhythm. The pain was excruciating. I didn't say a word and nor did he.

When he was finished, he climbed off and zipped up his trousers. Then he switched on the ignition. I pulled up my pants, and straightened my clothes. We drove back into the city in silence. He parked outside Kadesh and I got out of the car, unable to speak. He gave me a crooked smile, saying he would ring me later. I nodded my head, ashamed, confused, defeated.

I walked along the driveway, through the front door, past Amy's room on the right, past the chapel on the left, and up the stairs to my bedroom. It was Sunday and I could hear the nuns preparing dinner in the kitchen at the rear of the house. I hid in my room, trembling uncontrollably, waiting for the clatter to die down. I didn't want to see anyone but I needed a cup of coffee.

Finally I lay down, knowing sleep would never come; feeling hollow, feeling soulless, feeling violated. What had happened in the car seemed more than opportunism. More than a cheeky young man eyeing an innocent young woman on the footpath and chasing her down the road. This escapade seemed planned and plotted. His actions premeditated. He had me in his car. All to himself. Exactly where he wanted me. On a lonely dirt road, in the middle of nowhere.

There were no cuddles or kisses. No foreplay, no tenderness, no words. Perhaps he didn't know any better. But he stole my virginity as if it were nothing. That purity of body and soul that I was striving so hard to keep intact. That I was saving for God. Not that Carlos knew. I felt numb.

Three or four days passed. Then he rang, and I was scared. Strangely, because he had taken from me that which was most sacred, I felt worthless. I knew I shouldn't see him but the psychological effects of that first cruel sexual experience in his car had left me feeling brutalised and powerless to resist.

I wandered over to his house in a daze; disconnected, disassociated and dehumanised. He forced himself inside me again. Pinned me to the floor as pain ripped through me – mind and body locked in fright, speechless, defenceless.

If only I had had someone to confide in. If only something in my education or upbringing had prepared me in some way then it might have ended there, the harm minimized. But the only men I knew kept their hands to themselves and their trousers zipped up. The only men I knew were priests and seminarians. They were guarding their chastity and fighting to control their sexual urges as fiercely as I was.

But this man, Carlos, had stripped me of dignity. And I lay on the floor, naked. Legs covered in carpet burns. Broken beneath his will.

Chapter 13
The Retreat

All the young budding nuns in the States of Victoria and South Australia, myself included, had the opportunity of going on retreat – a time of prayer and meditation. I didn't want to go. I wanted to leave the Sacred Heart Order and go home to my parents.

I had told Amy I didn't have a religious vocation, but she insisted that I stay at Kadesh for a few more weeks, at least, and attend the retreat. So I acquiesced and obeyed. I was still respecting her position as Superior. Still letting her control me. Manipulate me. Silence me. Amy was hoping the retreat would change my mind and I would stay in the Order, but I knew it wouldn't.

On the third day of the retreat I decided to talk to the retreat leader, Father John McKeefry, who was from South Africa. He seemed trustworthy and I liked his gentle manner.

I waited until 8:30 pm before slipping outside unnoticed. Waves were crashing on the flat sandy beach nearby and the air was warm and salty. Father John's accommodation was in a separate wing, away from the main building. I knocked softly on his door and waited, looking over my shoulder, nervously.

"Hello, Maria. What can I do for you?" he asked.

He stood in the doorway, white hair shining in the half-light. He was dressed in black trousers with a gold cross on his white shirt collar. His voice sounded weary.

"Father, I need to talk to you. Is that all right?" I said.

"No, Maria. All conversations are to be shared with the group. We're here on this retreat together and we are trusting the process. Tomorrow at the group session, please."

Father John's voice was calm but firm and he moved to close the door in my face.

"That's impossible, Father," I replied quickly. "Absolutely impossible."

"You have to trust the group, Maria. That's the way it works."

"Please Father, I can't. I need to talk with you alone. There's no way I can share *this* with the group. Please!"

As a facilitator of healing and personal growth, Father John was leading us to trust self and to trust others. During a session the previous day I had witnessed uncontrollable sobbing and heartache. One of the young nuns was telling the tale of her miserable childhood in anger and resentment. Father John had handled the situation with sensitivity and composure and I'd been impressed. Still, I knew I couldn't share my problem with the group in an open forum.

We argued back and forth a little more but I was adamant. I would not be bullied.

"All right then," he conceded. "Come inside and take a seat."

I stepped into a dimly lit room. Books and pages of scrawled notes covered the coffee table.

He settled comfortably into his armchair. "Now Maria, what's all this about?"

"Father, I've got a problem," I said, scarcely daring to breathe. "I'm pregnant."

His eyes widened in shock but he remained quiet.

"I didn't go looking for someone, Father. It just happened that I met someone."

There… I'd said it. It was a start. I could breathe again. Slowly, deeply. There was no need to hurry to tell more. I hadn't thought through any particular strategy or choice of words. I was trusting the moment, simply and honestly.

"You don't look pregnant," Father John said.

"I am, believe me."

Slow deep breaths.

"If you're pregnant, why are you attending this retreat?" He sounded slightly annoyed.

It was a perfectly legitimate question and I knew it was absurd that I was attending a week-long retreat for aspiring nuns. I explained that my Superior hoped I would change my mind about leaving the convent. She didn't know I was pregnant.

"Had you ever been with a man before, Maria?"

"Of course not." I felt offended by the question.

"So how did it get to this?" Father John's voice had softened. He sounded sad. I felt wretched.

I told him about my life at Kadesh, about Amy, and Donna – trying to make sense of it. Becoming pregnant outside of wedlock was every Catholic girl's worst nightmare. But I wasn't a girl. I was a nun or, at least, a budding nun.

I talked about Father Jerome.

"Jerome's my only friend but he's old enough to be my father."

For two years I had quietly observed two religious communities from the side-lines. Now, words were starting to tumble out of my mouth because someone was listening. Soon I was babbling like a child telling tales to grandpa. But I didn't care. So much had been bottled up for so long. It had to come out.

Father peered over the top of his glasses. "But how on earth did it get to *this*, Maria?"

"I don't know, really. There's a strange atmosphere at Kadesh. The nuns seem burdened. There are very few new candidates coming forward to join their ranks. Added to that, three nuns have left the Order this year. It's affected everyone at Kadesh. Some of the nuns look depressed. Others live in their own private world, locked in their bedrooms. Maybe this has affected me. Maybe I've been too lonely, I don't know."

Father John watched me, cautiously.

"I'm having the baby adopted," I said, avoiding his gaze, feeling ashamed.

"Does the father know about the baby?"

"Yes. I told him immediately after the doctor confirmed the pregnancy."

I sensed I could trust Father John. So I told him about my first meeting with Carlos, about that first cup of coffee.

"You shouldn't have got into his car," he said. "You shouldn't have seen him again."

"I know."

We talked about me visiting Carlos at his home. I couldn't tell Father John about that first drive in the countryside. That memory, and other early memories, were unbearable and had been buried – which is where they would stay, forever.

"I have such a clear picture in my mind. Of lying on the carpet at his place. Of trying to hold his body off me. I told him to stop but he wouldn't listen."

"What do you mean, you told him to stop?"

The question hung between us.

"Just that," I sighed.

"Did he rape you?"

I shook my head from side to side. In horror, in disbelief.

"Did he rape you?"

I knew nothing about rape. And nothing about sex – not until I met Carlos. Surely, rape involved dark alleys, broken bottles, drugs, and prostitution. The punishment for rape was prison. I didn't wish that on him.

"You say you're going to have the baby adopted; why's that?"

I looked at him in dismay.

"Of course I'm having the baby adopted. I can't have a baby. It's impossible. I can't turn up in New Zealand with a baby in my arms. Everyone knows I've been training to become a nun."

I thought of the scandal it would cause. I thought of my parents, my siblings, my relations. I had been a part of the Catholic Church all my life. I knew that Catholic communities were not havens of forgiveness and love. They were small congregations of people with prejudices who gossiped, who accused and belittled.

"My parents are well known in the Catholic community in Auckland," I said, as if that added more weight to my decision.

I explained how Dad and Mother had worked tirelessly for the Church, organising some of the biggest events in the Catholic calendar. Dad had even saved Bishop Mackey's life when they capsized a dinghy as young boys. Bishop Mackey was the Bishop of Auckland.

"It's impossible, Father. I have to have the baby adopted. There's no other way. I intend to return to New Zealand and tell my parents. I'll swear them to secrecy so no one will ever know. Then I'll return to Australia and arrange the adoption here."

"Why's that, Maria?"

"It's what Catholic girls do in New Zealand. They hide in the countryside until after the birth, in shame, or they fly to Australia. Everyone knows that."

"Do they? Where will you stay when you return to Australia?"

"I have no idea. It'll be all right. I'll work it out."

"Secrets have a way of leaking out, you know."

"Don't worry. I'll swear my parents to secrecy. They'll never talk."

"Are you absolutely sure of that?"

"Oh yes, absolutely sure."

The conversation paused again, each of us locked in our own private thoughts.

"I'll have to visit the nuns at Kadesh. They're responsible for this, you know. Who's the Superior there?"

"No, you can't do that," I gasped. "They mustn't ever know."

"Who's the Superior? What's her name?"

"Amy," I replied. "Please, Father, don't."

"They've let you down. I'll be visiting them before I return to South Africa. I'll speak to the Superior and inform her of her total lack of care of you. This never should have happened to you. And that priest from the university," he said, thoughtfully, "he's responsible for awakening you – emotionally."

I shook my head from side to side. 'Awakening me emotionally.' What did that mean? Jerome had tried to be a friend, nothing more.

"But Father, they mustn't ever know. Please don't." My stomach was knotting in fear.

"Don't worry. I won't tell them about the pregnancy but they have to be reprimanded for failing to look after you. It was their responsibility. They had a duty of care and they let you down atrociously. Religious communities are meant to be places of love, understanding, peace and harmony. You should have felt supported and protected, Maria. This never should have happened to you."

I imagined him standing in the front entrance at Kadesh. Would Amy open the door?

"What will you do after the baby is born? Have you thought of that?" he asked.

"I really don't know. For the last few years I've been focused on the idea of vocation, of becoming a nun."

"But you don't have a vocation, Maria." He spoke with authority.

"I don't know, maybe I do," I shrugged.

"You do *not* have a vocation."

"How do you know that? Janet, one of the nuns at Kadesh, told me the other day that she thinks I do."

"If you did, this never would have happened to you."

I didn't understand.

He asked permission to share my predicament with Sister Maureen, who was his assistant on the retreat. He assured me she was trustworthy.

It was dark by the time I left his rooms. I felt relieved that all the lights were off in the main building and everyone was fast asleep in the dormitory. I wouldn't have to dread any questions.

An hour later I heard a voice at the curtain to my cubicle and Sister Maureen entered. The softness of her words in the darkness brought tears to my eyes and my body shook with emotion as she cradled me in her arms. I had shed only one or two tears in silence after returning from the doctor's appointment a few weeks before, never again allowing myself any expression of emotion or self-pity.

Finally, the seriousness and sadness of my situation hit me and I cried. I listened to Sister Maureen's soothing voice, offering comfort and support. She would help me, she whispered. She would find me somewhere to live in Melbourne. Everything would be all right.

At the end of the retreat I returned to Kadesh and promptly told Amy that I still wanted to leave the Order. She booked and paid for my flight home to New Zealand because I had no money. After two years in the convent I was going home to my parents – poor, needy and pregnant.

I visited Carlos and tried to discuss the future, the baby, and all the options. I felt sure I had only one real option. I outlined my intention of going home to New Zealand for Christmas and then returning to Australia in the New Year, to arrange an adoption.

"Who have you been talking to?" Carlos shouted.

I was surprised at his anger because I was only repeating what I'd said before. I mentioned abortion and in the same breath I ruled it out. I believed every child was a child of God, with a soul. I believed God was in charge of creation and that I had no right to question that process. For me, abortion amounted to murder. In New Zealand I had been actively involved in supporting a Pro-Life parliamentary candidate who had lived with my family in the lead-up to the 1975 general election. I had attended Pro-Life rallies, singing songs on stage with my brothers. I had stood outside the first abortion clinic in New Zealand, holding banners and praying silently. Despite my predicament, I couldn't ignore my respect for the unborn child.

But raising a child on my own, being a solo mother, that would never be my choice. Neither for my child nor for me.

"You tell me what you want to do," I said.

Carlos was sulky, refusing to talk. I stayed the night with him, the first and only time. I wanted an answer from him because I was leaving for New Zealand in a few days.

Later that night he confirmed what I already knew: adoption was the only feasible option. The next morning I returned to the convent, knowing that no one would have even noticed my absence.

I phoned my parents and told them I would be home for Christmas. They, of course, were excited. I let them think everything was wonderful.

A few days later they met me at Auckland airport. We visited family and friends in the city before driving to their new home, north of Auckland. It was 11 pm before we arrived home, too late to talk. Dad and Mother went to bed, happy and relaxed. I counted the hours till dawn.

There was so much to think about. Four years had slipped by since that Saturday morning in confession. Mother had tried to dissuade me from listening to Father McSweeney but I had been willing to take up the challenge and begin the journey to become a nun. Now I would have to tell her the mess I was in. I knew it would break her heart.

Chapter 14
A Mother's Fears

Mother screamed with horror when I told her I was pregnant. She was sitting in an armchair in the lounge, surrounded by all the medical gadgets she needed to control her asthma. A tank of oxygen, a face-mask, a ventilator and bottles of medicine. She reached for her inhaler, her body shaking uncontrollably. My news was bringing on an asthma attack. I felt dreadful.

"If I don't get married I'm having the baby adopted," I said, trying to sound confident.

"What? You can't do that." Mother was hysterical – exactly the reaction I expected. "You can't give up your baby. It's not right. You'll never be able to do it. You don't understand about motherhood."

The lounge walls were covered in religious icons, all sad and depressing. The Sacred Heart of Jesus crowned with thorns had pride of place in the centre of the main wall. Hanging alongside was the Immaculate Heart of Mary pierced with an arrow. And, on another wall, the figure of Christ on the cross, Our Lady of Fatima crying tears of blood, and Padre Pio raising his stigmatised hand in a blessing. A collection of photos of miraculous statues from around the world – all revealing more tears of blood – hung side by side above the glass doors in the dining room.

Most of the pictures were familiar to me but there were a few new ones, bloodier and more grotesque. They dominated the walls in the open-plan living area. I thought it excessive and, if I had been at home, I would have tried to moderate Mother's behaviour like I usually did. But I had been gone two years. She had everything in her new house exactly where she wanted it. Not one of her six children had been there to argue or protest or interfere. And Dad, her passive and peace-seeking companion, allowed her to have her own way, giving tacit approval.

"I'm suffering just like the Sorrowful Mother," she sobbed. "I've offered my life to God as a victim soul. Only God knows how much I suffer. But I'm doing it to save sinners. Without victim souls the whole world is going to hell. And all my children are going to hell, too. Who would have thought that I would have children like this? You're just the same as all the others. Sometimes I wish I'd never married."

Her voice trembled with emotion as she wiped tears from her face.

"Another sword of sorrow to pierce my heart!" she gasped. "You children are killing me!"

My heart sank. I remained quiet while she vented. I had heard it all so many times before but the difference was that, this time, it was directed at me.

"You watch! I'll be dead soon and then you'll all be sorry you didn't listen to your mother."

She glanced at Dad who was drying the lunch dishes, a look of disgust on her face. She blamed him. She always blamed him for any perceived weaknesses and shortcomings in her children. Dad never retaliated. He saw no need. He loved her and he knew she loved him.

Her health seemed worse than ever. She was a pathetic figure; choking, spluttering, wheezing and snivelling. Medication no longer helped. Suddenly I was profoundly aware that I had to protect my baby from her interference and influence. I saw myself as a brave young woman, able to cope with a difficult mother. But I resolved to do everything in my power to ensure that my child would never experience any of the emotional hysteria or religious fanaticism that had dominated our home life. That type of hysteria and fanaticism had driven my siblings away.

Dad never interrupted as I continued my story about Kadesh, Father Jerome and Father John. I shielded them from any facts that would have discredited Carlos in any way, thereby laying all the blame on me. They listened, utterly horrified.

Once they were over the initial shock, I talked to them of happier things. I tried to soften the blow by talking about Carlos with affection. As the afternoon slipped by, Mother's asthma abated and Dad's face brightened up. The worst was over for the moment.

The next day Mother looked better after a good night's sleep. Dad was back to his usual self, quiet and unflustered, but he couldn't hide his deep disappointment in me. I had studied his face all my life and could read his every wrinkle.

After breakfast we drove to Puhoi to go to Mass at the church of Saints Peter and Paul. Nothing had changed in Puhoi in my absence; in fact, Puhoi hadn't changed in a hundred years. The small township in a farming district of fat cows and lush green pastures consisted of little more than a post office and grocery store, pub and disused school and convent, now all badly dilapidated. An old wooden church with colourful stained-glass windows nestled comfortably in the centre of the historic village, and an elderly priest fitted perfectly into the tranquillity. His congregation was tiny during the weekdays, with only two or three old ladies plus my parents.

After Mass we returned home and discussions continued again around the dining room table.

"You're not giving the baby up for adoption," Mother said. She and Dad had obviously been discussing the situation overnight. "We'll look after the baby, Dad and I."

This was a strong statement from a petite woman with a huge heart and a deep commitment to her God. Society still expected young mothers to be married and illegitimate babies to be adopted by childless couples who would provide decent homes and stability. Christian Churches, especially the Catholic Church, frowned on unmarried mothers in their congregations. Such women symbolised depravity and loose morals. If an unmarried woman was unlucky enough, or stupid enough, to get pregnant then she was expected to marry the father or give up the baby for adoption. It was her duty to do so. Mother's offer to care for my baby, despite the gossip and humiliation, was testament to her love for me and my unborn child; and proof of her overriding sense of duty.

"No, Mother, that won't happen," I replied. "This is my decision and I know adoption is the best option."

"Eddie, what do you think?"

"I'll support Maria in whatever decision she makes," he replied. I was relieved Dad had taken my side over Mother's: that didn't happen often.

I sat in the dining room, looking composed, yet hiding all my emotions. Feeling sad and sorry for myself wouldn't have achieved anything. I recalled Father John's compassion which had allowed me to confide in him and I compared his response to Mother's. She could be hot-blooded and bad-tempered when she wanted to be. She believed in a God who demanded retribution – and so did she. I didn't expect any sympathy from her.

I reminded myself that God turns everything to good for those who love Him. It was my favourite passage from St Paul's Letters to the Romans. My Faith remained firm despite the difficult position I was in. God was still my Creator and Saviour.

Thankfully, Mother knew she couldn't force her will on me. She had done so many times in the past, and against strong opposition but, this time, she didn't have any power. This was my body, my baby, my decision.

Once Mother had had time to adjust her thinking she resigned herself to the inevitability of adoption, although she never accepted the idea. For her, motherhood was precious. God was involved in the creative process, and mother and baby belonged together, despite everything. She saw every baby as a soul for God, a soul that needed to be saved. She expected me to shoulder my responsibilities.

Over the next few weeks, the red clock on the kitchen windowsill ticked mechanically as the peacefulness of their rural lifestyle penetrated my every pore, allowing me to reconnect with my old self. Dad, Mother and I knew how to get on together. And, strange as it may seem, I began to sense that Mother was proud of me. I was carrying a baby and, in her opinion, fulfilling a woman's noblest vocation.

Their house was the only dwelling on a private road. Built on a knoll, it overlooked a steep valley covered in dense native bush on one side and farmland on the other. A lazy, meandering river flowed right past the property.

Each day we went to Mass together, the three of us, and after Mass we weeded the vegetable and flower gardens. Dad set the possum traps and cured possum furs. He sharpened his chainsaw, ready for use. He was working his way through felling hundreds of trees. Mother baked. She wouldn't let me walk up and down the steep hillside to the muddy bay at the bottom of the property to set the fishing net. It was a job I had enjoyed the previous summer. She thought it too strenuous, my wading in mud with a sack of fish slung over my shoulder. So I got out the weaving loom to make some cushion covers for the lounge and Mother sat at her spinning wheel, treadling. On the surface, life was simple and happy.

A few weeks later I flew back to Melbourne, accompanied by Dad. He wanted to see me settled into a flat. Five months later he returned with Mother for the birth.

In the meantime I had readjusted into my new life. Sister Maureen had kept her word and found me somewhere to live. My health was good; no morning sickness, no stress, and no contact with Carlos.

I stayed out of sight, hidden from everyone and everything I'd ever known. Conscious of the wonder of the baby inside – a baby that was mine to nurture for only nine months – I waited for the birth.

Chapter 15
Yellow Daffodils

The waiting was over with the onset of winter. I had been in hospital all night, hoping it wasn't a false alarm, willing the contractions to increase in severity. But they didn't.

"Maria, the doctor has decided to keep you in because the baby is already a week overdue," the nurse said. "If nothing happens by midday we'll perform an amniotomy, or breaking of the bag of amniotic fluid. It's a simple procedure and you shouldn't feel anything. It should start things rolling along nicely. Are you okay with that? Any questions?"

"That's fine," I said.

The room was well-lit, with sparkling floors and shiny stainless steel equipment – medical equipment, ready for use. I was ready, too. I was tired of hanging around, biding time, hiding, and leading a secret life.

"Put your feet up, dear. That usually helps," the nurse said kindly.

Did she know I was an unmarried mother? I looked at the gold band I was wearing on my ring finger. I had bought it some months before, when Sister Maureen arranged accommodation for me with a young family she knew. I had fabricated a story about my husband being overseas in order to avoid awkward questions. The ring gave credence to that story.

I wondered what was on my medical notes. Was there anything about adoption? Had she read the notes?

"If you need anything, press the bell."

"Thanks, I will."

She left the room. I sat on the bed with my feet on a footstool. I had plenty of time to think. There was no need to panic. Women had been giving birth since the beginning of time. It was all perfectly natural. I wasn't the least bit concerned.

The act of conception seemed so bizarre and random. It wasn't necessarily tied up with love at all, yet a baby could be conceived – and so easily. Why would something as precious as the creation of new life be designed by God, an all-powerful God, to be so invisible and elusive?

My parents had arrived in Melbourne three weeks earlier. We were staying at a motel along the road from the hospital. Mother had bundled me off to hospital at midnight the previous night with the first signs of contractions. Dad had accompanied me in a taxi but I sent him back to the motel, confident I was fine on my own.

I poured myself a glass of water and thought about the advice the adoption counsellor had given me. She said that after the birth, on my return to New Zealand, I should pretend nothing had ever happened. She said I would meet a charming young man and that I would get married and live happily ever after. Life would be wonderful, all would be well. I didn't believe her. How could I? Nothing like that had happened to me before. So how and why would it magically happen now?

Now that I'd ruined my life? And besides, the counsellor was a nun. What did she know about life or men? Probably nothing.

At midday the nurse broke the bag of amniotic fluid. I was taken to the birthing suite to endure the pain of childbirth, which was much worse than I had expected, but I had wanted to feel it all naturally, drug-free. I wasn't going to have the experience of motherhood but no one could deny me the experience of child birth, undiluted.

Later that afternoon, I gave birth to a son.

"He's perfect," the doctor said with delight as he held him high in the air. "Absolutely perfect."

The baby screamed.

"Would you like to have baby in bed with you for a minute or two?" a nurse asked.

"Yes," I nodded, exhausted.

She laid him down beside me, face to face. I talked to him quietly and he screamed again. Everyone left the room and the nurse picked him up and carried him away without a word. I lay there alone, feeling empty.

The next day I rang Carlos. Months of suppressed emotion welled up inside and I cried uncontrollably into the phone. I wanted Carlos to come to the hospital and sign the adoption papers, naming him as the birth father, but he refused. I tried again the next day and the next, heartbroken and tearful. He remained immovable. The illegal immigrant was determined to protect his anonymity.

Mother was anxious to see the baby before I left the hospital and so I asked that he be brought to my room. She unwrapped his clothing, admiring his perfect little limbs. She adored babies. I thought he was a miracle but he wasn't mine to have. Dad looked on, smiling. He had a cuddle, too. This was their seventh grandchild, the one they thought they would never see again.

We wandered around Melbourne for the next week, counting the hours. Milk stains stopped soaking through my clothes, leaving the pain and bruising of an episiotomy as the only reminders of my sad ordeal. Mother watched me closely, fearful that my newly enlarged breasts wouldn't reduce in time for me to return to New Zealand without causing suspicion.

One cold frosty morning, about two weeks after the birth, I walked along the road to the hospital to sign the adoption papers. I was carrying a bouquet of bright yellow daffodils and dainty white gypsophila to give to the adoption counsellor whose mother had just died. Mother insisted that I take the flowers, which she wrapped in layers of clear cellophane, tied with white satin ribbons. We wrote on a sympathy card. It was a typical Mother gesture: always thinking of others, being charitable, and putting 'self last'.

However, deep inside, I knew I didn't want to take flowers to the counsellor. And I told Mother so. For me it was wrong. What about my loss? It was much greater than the counsellor's but it had to go unacknowledged. It had to be squashed. I knew the daffodils were yet another memory that I would have to bury forever.

Although the laws around adoption in the state of Victoria allowed me to have an 'open adoption' with full access to my son, I resolved never to make any contact with him or his adoptive parents. I had decided it would be too painful. My love was the same as my mother's and my grandmother's: intense, heartfelt, and all-consuming.

A few days later my parents and I landed at Auckland Airport. We walked through the exit holding our heads high, smiling cheerfully. We were putting on a show for my youngest brother, Joe, who was meeting us.

"What have you been doing with yourself all these months?" Joe asked as we walked to the car.

Dark, thunderous clouds threatened the winter sky. I'd missed those clouds. It felt good to be home.

"I've been working in a parish with migrant families," I lied. "Mostly Italians, Greeks and South Africans."

"Sounds interesting," he replied.

He seemed relaxed and I sensed he suspected nothing. So I developed that storyline further, making it sound like I'd made the progression from budding nun to ex-nun without any difficulty and, in the process, I convinced myself I could silence even the most inquisitive minds.

After spending a couple of weeks at Puhoi with my parents, I moved down to Auckland to live with Joe who was house-minding and attending university. I got a temporary job, working as a clerk for a government department, while waiting for the release of the next *Teachers' Gazette* which advertised the teaching jobs for the new year.

I told myself to put the past behind me and toughen up. There was no other way. But I was lonely. I had no friends in New Zealand and I was wary of all priests and nuns, just in case someone knew something about me. I had a secret that must never be shared, not even with my siblings.

A couple of months later my parents started visiting my brother and me in Auckland, taking over the spare bedroom for days at a time. Mother assumed control of the kitchen, which gave her the perfect opportunity to reassert herself as queen bee. We watched, helplessly, as our independence and freedom vanished.

We learnt that our parents had decided to sell their property and move back to Auckland, to set up house again for Joe and me. Their reasons were threefold: they missed the family, they'd upset the locals, and their plans for building a Catholic retirement village had met with too many obstacles, making the venture impossible. However, I was desperate to keep them in Puhoi. I loved their rural hideaway and I wanted time to readjust without their interference.

Even though I knew instinctively how to protect my baby from Mother's influence, I didn't have a clue about myself. Mother quoted the fourth commandment, tirelessly: *Honour your father and your mother.*

I quoted St Paul's Letter to the Colossians, Chapter 3:21: *Parents, do not drive your children to resentment.*

I was joined to my parents even more deeply than before but I was in a peculiar space, and full of denial. I didn't feel comfortable with the new Maria. She had broken the rules. I didn't know who she was or where she fitted in. She wasn't a virgin but she was pretending to be one. She was a mother but she had no baby.

In the New Year I started teaching at a school in South Auckland called Nga Tapuwae College (NTC). I put on a brave face each day at school. NTC was a Maori community college, recently built in response to the rapidly expanding Maori and Polynesian population that was filling the need for unskilled labour.

The staff at NTC were young and enthusiastic, some just married with new-borns and toddlers. I was the white girl with the private school education, with all the advantages that money could buy, with the Christian principles and the posh accent – an accent I was keen to lose.

Sitting in the staffroom at morning tea and lunchtime, I was detached and wary. It wasn't difficult to imagine the gossip, the raised eyebrows, the sniggering if anyone got a whiff of my time in Melbourne. Ex-nun. Unplanned pregnancy. Adopted baby. I needed time to heal.

At home, life with Mother was trying. She treated Joe and me like children, insisting we obey her in everything. I slipped back into my old role of listening to her woes and trying to console and appease her. I didn't know what else to do.

During the previous four years I had learnt to silence myself as I focused on emptying myself of all desires in order for God to lead me. Part of that process entailed waiting, but the waiting was over now, although I was conditioned to waiting – on God, and then for a baby's birth. Being a teacher was the easy bit. Having a sense of self, of purpose, integrated with the past while looking to the future, was problematic.

I had to turn my attention away from God and away from religious vocation. I had to make some friends other than Jesus. But how?

Eventually I decided to join the Saint Augustine Club, a Catholic singles club in Auckland. It seemed like a good place to start. However, when I walked into the venue I recognised only one person in the room: the priest who was running it. Not surprisingly I was nervous, wondering what he knew about me. And I felt like a fraud. I was second-hand goods, old beyond my years, and I quickly convinced myself that no one would want to know me. I made an early exit, resolving never to return.

Six months later I met Sebastian, a man twenty years my senior. Mother was horrified at the age difference. Dad was pleased to see me moving on. And I was grateful Sebastian didn't ask any awkward questions.

This was the first intimate relationship I had willingly participated in. A simple case of trying to behave like an adult while being led by a man almost twice my age. He was a widower with a grown-up family.

Although we weren't madly in love we shared some good times. He brought friendship and normality to my world, and put some distance between me and my past. Nevertheless, my conscience struggled with a new dilemma: whether to remain a traditional Catholic and obey the old rules or to scrap the rules and become a modern young woman. The second option involved reprogramming my conscience, rewriting the rules and, therefore, disobeying the Pope – God's representative on earth.

I was bewildered by my past. I had trusted God but He hadn't protected me. He had let me down and I got hurt. Now I had no virginity to protect, no vow of chastity to aspire to, but an opportunity to grow. It was a starting point, one I decided on alone – I had no friends to guide or reassure me. My version of Catholicism evolved into a combination of old and new ideas.

Unprotected sex in Sebastian's car on Saturday night, with early withdrawal, was extremely dangerous and nerve-racking. I was breaking the rules and taking an unnecessary risk because I still couldn't use contraception – doing so would have involved an even bigger shift in my thinking, and I wasn't yet ready for that level of freedom and self-determination.

I didn't get pregnant again – miraculously or luckily. Maybe, like many other women who have given away a baby, my hurt was so deep that my body shut down, saving me from further trauma.

I ended the relationship with Sebastian on the phone one day at school, after discovering by pure chance that he had lied to me and taken an older woman to a family wedding. Apparently, I was too young to meet that branch of the family. My rage exploded, fuelled by stifling my voice at Loreto Hall and Kadesh, by being violated by Carlos, and giving away my baby.

I lashed out at Sebastian in an ugly outpouring of injustice and resentment, forbidding him from ever ringing me again. Then I slammed the phone down, without giving him the chance of reply.

At the end of that term, a long winter's term, I drove home from school, tired and disillusioned.

Chapter 16
Apparitions and Ecstasies

August in Auckland is often cold and blustery, and August 1980 was no different from any other year. Both fires at home were blazing – the potbelly in the living room and the open fire in the conversation pit.

All I wanted after a busy term of teaching was a little peace and quiet; except Mother had to interfere. She had been hounding me all week but I had managed to resist. Now she pounced, placing a religious newspaper on the table in front of me.

"Read it," she said. "I just got it from a nun I know. It's about a new place of religious apparitions in Southern Spain, in a village called Palmar de Troya."

She sounded excited – apparitions were one of her favourite topics – but I wasn't interested. I just wanted to sort out my life.

We were living in a new house in Mariner's Cove, on Auckland's North Shore. It was a fun house to live in, with seven levels, purple carpet, and sea views. We should have been having fun, but I had a secret that wouldn't go away while Mother couldn't stop being Mother. Even Dad's boats, a twenty-two foot fibreglass yacht named *Alpha*, and a forty-five foot Ferro-cement schooner named *Beachcomber*, moored at the bottom of the cliff nearby didn't give us the impetus we needed to live life differently.

Mother still felt responsible for my salvation because I was living at home. Joe had a legitimate excuse not to read anything as he was studying for exams, but I was on holiday, right under her nose, and idle.

Outside, squalls of rain lashed the window panes. I put more wood in the potbelly and stoked the fire, scouring my brain for excuses, trying to stall the inevitable. Mother was in good form this week, her asthma under control. She was back to her old self: motivated and energised. What chance did I have?

I opened the paper and read. The article stated that in 1968 four children said that Mary, the Mother of God, had appeared to them on a hillside as they picked flowers for an altar at school. This was the reason they gave their parents for coming home late that day.

Nothing new there, I thought.

The story continued in typical fashion with the Virgin Mary asking the young children to pray and do penance.

Pilgrimages to holy places were actively encouraged by the Church hierarchy. Every year Catholics and non-Catholics flocked in their thousands to Lourdes in France and Fatima in Portugal, seeking healing in body and soul.

However, more recently there had been reports of various new places of apparition: at Garabandal in Spain, San Damiano in Italy and Bayside in New York. Thousands of people believed that they were authentic too, even though the Church had not officially declared them to be so. Historically, the Vatican moved very slowly in condemning or approving places of apparition, but, in the meantime, Catholics were free to believe or not as they so wished.

The story of Palmar de Troya appeared to follow the same path as these other apparitions, with the same recurring themes of doom and gloom: the Church was in crisis, priests were leading sinful lives, and God was angry.

I focused on finding the facts. I needed Mother to stop nagging.

"Coffee, darling?" she asked. "The scones are nearly ready."

How could I say 'no'?

Over the next hour I kept reading.

The news of Mary's appearance to the four children of Palmar de Troya spread like wildfire through their tiny village. Other villagers soon accompanied the children to the place where Mary had supposedly appeared to them. They went there to pray, hoping Mary would come again. As more people gathered on the hillside, others experienced wonderful ecstasies too – seeing visions, hearing heavenly messages and smelling exquisite perfumes.

"Some of the visionaries have received the stigmata," I said, somewhat surprised.

"I know," Mother replied.

"There are photos here, showing wounds in their hands and feet. And even a crown of thorns on one person."

"Just like Padre Pio."

Mother sounded triumphant. She loved Padre Pio, the Italian Capuchin priest from Pietrelcina (1887–1968). During his life he was famous for having received similar graces from God, including the gifts of levitation, bi-location, and reading souls. Magazines had often reported stories of movie stars and wives of important politicians visiting him in confession.

I flicked over to the next page. Reporters and cameramen had done a fine job of recording the seemingly miraculous events at Palmar de Troya. Busloads of tourists from all over Europe, totalling forty thousand on one occasion, had created a lot of hype. Some pilgrims were quoted as having witnessed the spinning of the sun, like at Fatima in 1917. Others said they witnessed miracles; the sick were healed.

"Apparently, the Archbishop of the Catholic Church in Seville condemned the apparitions and heavenly messages as superstitious and, therefore, damaging to the Faith," I said.

"Yes, but he didn't carry out an official enquiry or question any of the seers," Mother replied, sternly. "And that's contrary to Church law. Little wonder some of the believers doubled their efforts to promote the apparitions. I would have done the same, if I'd been in their shoes."

I didn't doubt that.

One group of believers travelled through Europe and South America to promote the apparitions. They even visited Pope Paul VI in Rome. On one of these journeys, a young man from Seville called

Clemente, who was one of the main visionaries, was involved in a serious car accident.

"Did you know Clemente lost his eyes in an accident?"

"No, I didn't," Mother replied. "I haven't got that far yet."

"He's completely blind now, poor guy."

"Show me."

I walked into the kitchen, holding the paper up for her to see.

"Gosh! He looks terrible," she said, staring at the empty eye sockets and closed lids.

"Apparently, he's very charismatic."

"Keep reading."

I didn't need encouraging. Clemente had admitted to having led a sinful life. I could relate to that.

A large donation from a wealthy Spanish dowager enabled him to buy the hillside on which the first apparitions took place. Then plans were drawn up for the construction of a cathedral, and foundations laid.

In 1975 Clemente formed a religious order called the Carmelites of the Holy Face (of Jesus) believing that God had spoken to him in a vision. Although the Order didn't have official approval from Rome, it claimed to be faithful to Pope Paul VI who, metaphorically speaking, was considered to be a prisoner in the Vatican – a rumour that had been circulating in traditional Catholic circles for several years.

In 1976 Ngo Dinh Thuc, a Vietnamese Archbishop and brother of the President of the

Republic of Vietnam who had been assassinated in 1963, ordained Clemente and his friend, Manuel, to the priesthood. After their ordination he made them bishops, together with three other priests. More ordinations followed. Although they were subsequently excommunicated by Pope Paul VI, Thuc considered that since the Church was in The Last Times, mandatory authorisation from Rome was not required. Thuc also believed that the Pope secretly supported Clemente and his followers.

"When Pope Paul VI died in 1978, Clemente had a vision of himself being crowned Pope by Jesus," I continued. "He claims that Jesus transferred the Papacy from Rome to Palmar de Troya."

Mother sat down beside me, all ears.

"Clemente took the name Gregory XVII. He's established his own College of Cardinals. He thinks John Paul I was an Anti-Pope."

I glanced up from the newspaper, horrified.

John Paul I had died within a month of his coronation – such a short reign for a Pope. At the time we wondered why there had been no autopsy, except Vatican protocol made no allowances for such things.

Conversations around our dinner table had been tense as we revelled in the intrigue and mystery of a possible Vatican assassin. However, as soon as John Paul II was elected, we knew the secrets of the Vatican would never be uncovered.

"Maybe his death was at the hand of God," Mother said.

"Not an assassination as we thought?"

"We need more information," she said, getting up. "Set the table, darling, and call Dad. He's in the wood shed. Dinner's ready."

It was nearly dark outside. I switched on the lights, folded the newspaper, and put it aside. I'd read enough for the moment. My head was buzzing.

Later that night, and for several consecutive days and nights, we spent every spare moment reading. As Dad caught up with the storyline, discussions became more focused.

The Church had modernised, true enough. The rules were relaxed. The concept of sin had changed. But had God really abandoned Rome in place of Palmar de Troya? That one question dominated our thoughts. If the incredible stories emerging from the remote village of Southern Spain were anything to go by, then it did seem plausible.

Over the next few months we continued reading a wide range of books on Church history. Mother bought subscriptions to various overseas newspapers, including *L'Osservatore Romano,* the semi-official newspaper of the Vatican. Yet, the more we read, the more questions we had, causing us to narrow our focus in search of answers. While Dad and I tried to fend off Mother's fixation to unravel the truth, we braced ourselves against the effects of the steroids which had altered her personality and made her aggressive and unreasonable.

Whenever the rest of the family came to visit, simple discussions quickly escalated into heated arguments about religion. After a few such visits, the family stopped coming, but the discussions at home continued.

If the Pope is infallible when speaking on matters of Faith and Morals (by virtue of the promise Jesus made to Peter in St Mathew 16:18) then traditional Catholics were right to question the Church for seemingly breaking its own rules. On the other hand, Vatican Council II had opened the windows, and let the Holy Spirit in – hence the changes.

Eager to understand the extent to which new theology was influencing the next generation of young priests in Auckland, Dad and Mother started attending Mass at other parishes. In speaking to young priests they discovered that not one of them had ever heard the word 'transubstantiation', the process whereby a small wafer becomes the body, blood, soul and divinity of Jesus during the Consecration at Mass. Transubstantiation is at the very heart of Catholicism.

"What's happened to our Faith?" Mother asked. "It's gone!"

Dad wrote to the Bishop of Auckland but he dismissed our concerns. Then my parents spoke to the local priest, but he was too preoccupied with a recent health scare to give them any serious time.

Dire headlines in Catholic newspapers continued to report stories of hundreds of thousands of Catholics leaving the Church. Some flocked to Archbishop Lefebvre in France who was a traditionalist.

Belief in Jesus is based, in part, on His power to perform miracles. Without miracles, would Jesus ever have been hailed 'Son of God'? Probably not. And, just as the 'feeding of the five thousand' was seen as a sign from God, Palmar de Troya seemed to provide proof that God was, indeed, at work.

Another bout of bronchial asthma kept Mother in bed for weeks, giving her unlimited time to read and pray. Unfortunately for Dad and me, once recovered, she climbed out of bed, ready to face us again, armed with more evidence.

"What kind of Catholics are we?" she demanded.

Dad was thoughtful. I was listening. My secret was never far from my mind – buried but not forgotten – of dreams shattered and a baby abandoned. For Dad and Mother, a daughter's life was ruined, a grandchild lost. There was no going back, no fix, but plenty of time to reflect and repent.

"We mustn't forget Jesus' words: '*Because you are lukewarm, neither hot nor cold, I will begin to vomit you out of my mouth,*'" she said, referencing Revelations 3:16 – one of her favourite quotations.

Dad and I glanced at one another. Were we lukewarm?

Mother never tolerated a half-hearted approach to anything, especially our commitment to God and His Church. And she loved to remind us that Jesus felt the same way.

"Do we have the courage of our convictions?" she asked.

Yes, of course we do.

She was hot on the scent of truth, fixated and emboldened, hunting her prize. Dad and I were caught in the chase. After the confusion and failure of the past few years, I was ready to believe in something new, and the apparitions at Palmar de Troya filled that need.

Chapter 17
The Pact

The sun tipped over the horizon and rolled like a molten ball of fiery lava onto the Chicago skyline. It was 5.00 am.

"Are you awake?" His voice was flat, detached.

I stared at the back of his head. He was seated in the front of the car. He seemed like a stranger and I didn't think I liked him.

"Yes," I replied.

He had come to New Zealand on a business trip for a week, having made contact with Mother through the Palmarian printing centre in Ireland. He brought a collection of photos of Palmar de Troya, and challenged our commitment to Pope Gregory XVII. He impressed us with his enthusiasm and then, the day before he left, he asked me out on a date. After a romantic dinner he invited me to visit him in Wisconsin, with a view to marriage.

Tall, handsome, and blond he looked like he belonged in Hollywood. And the amazing thing was that he wanted me. Surely, only God could make such magic happen.

Now, after eight weeks of long-distance phone calls, the bouquets of red roses he'd sent had died, and the promise of happiness was about to descend on me with all its wonder.

I thought he would pick me up, swirl me around, bury his face in mine. Instead, when he met me at the airport, he barked, "What's that? Take it off."

He was pointing at the white fur coat I was wearing.

"I've just come from winter," I said.

"You don't need it. It's summer here."

He sounded gruff and bossy. But why? Only forty-eight hours earlier he had been laughing and joking on the phone, like he did every night, impressing me with his wit, his charm. And now, this.

We had waited in his car at the airport for a few hours because my luggage was arriving on another flight. But I couldn't sleep in the car. *What's that? Take it off* repeated in my head – the voice ugly, the words cruel.

His mood improved as we drove out of the airport car park, leaving behind the grey of big city Chicago for the golden plains of the mid-west. Eight hours later we arrived at his place.

"Maria, lovely to meet you at last, my dear," his mum said, hugging me warmly. She sounded genuine.

He looked like his mum but he had his father's temperament, his siblings later confided. I had *my* father's temperament – calm, steady, patient. I knew how to accommodate an irascible temper.

Give it time, I thought.

Over the next few weeks he maintained a happy mood as we went biking, tramping, golfing, swimming and boating. Autumn came quickly and we went ice-skating. Snowflakes fell and deer stepped out of the forest and onto the back lawn.

Each morning I drove to the Palmarian chapel in the woods and prayed alone. On Sundays he joined the congregation, fulfilling his religious obligation. The all-American boy, who had presented so well in New Zealand, didn't need to impress me anymore. His religious commitment started and stopped with his cheque book.

Five weeks later he said, "I don't love you. You can go home."

We were sitting side by side on the sofa – but not touching – in the downstairs apartment where I was staying. There was always a space between us, and now I knew why. The words were simple, the message clear but brutal.

"Surely you knew there was a chance this would never work?"

I remembered the airport. How could I forget?

"Your mum, my mum, the letters, the plan to meet you, the fake business trip," he added.

"What are you talking about?"

"Oh! Come on! You knew it was a set-up."

I shook my head from side to side, frowning. How could Mother do this to me? Why didn't Dad stop her?

"I'm going upstairs," he said. He wanted to get away.

I sat on the sofa alone till well past midnight.

I hadn't known he was single until the last night of his New Zealand trip. The dinner date, the romance, the invitation to visit him in America had happened so fast. There was no time to dawdle, procrastinate or dither. He'd wanted an answer then and there. He was decisive, articulate and convincing.

I knew that as a Palmarian Catholic I could only marry a Palmarian. And here was someone giving me a chance to make a new start, to build a relationship and have a family. It was impossible to resist.

Mother must have been concerned about my future. But why not discuss it with me? I had moved on from teaching and was studying singing full-time; it was a step in a new direction. Of course, she knew I would never agree to a blind date or an arranged marriage. But why interfere in the first place?

I didn't sleep that night or the next, I felt so betrayed and belittled.

But his family loved me. They wanted me.

"Don't go, not yet," they whispered.

But what was the point of staying?

"He says you pull up your skirt when biking," his mother shared. "And you lean over the handlebars to reveal your breasts."

My breasts! My blouse was buttoned to the neck. Surely, she saw the shock on my face. What a clever ploy, though, to insinuate that I was throwing myself at him, inappropriately.

"That's the reason he called it off," she continued.

I was speechless.

What a joke! And worse…What a liar! He didn't dare tell his mum he didn't love me. Not after all the fuss. Not after all the phone calls which must have cost him thousands. Everyone else loved me. Why couldn't he?

As the temperature dropped to 10 below, I moved in with one of his siblings.

"Give him time," they pleaded.

But what about my past? I'd never be able to tell him. He wouldn't understand and he wouldn't forgive me. And what about the scar from the episiotomy? There was no hiding that.

Four weeks later I caught a flight home. As soon as the plane left the runway at Madison Airport, tears fell uncontrollably. Everything was broken.

Back home in New Zealand I unpacked my suitcase for the eighth time in eight years. Inside, the emptiness was unbearable and I turned to God, with a new intensity, to show me a way forward. Still, never for a moment did I expect to receive a direct message from Him. So, when I heard a voice one day, I didn't know what to think.

I had gone back to teaching, although only relieving. I was tired after a long day. Was I confused, too?

"*Will you make reparation?*" the voice said.

I was in my bedroom and turned around to check the stairwell. There was definitely no one else there – only Mother in the kitchen downstairs.

I focused on the voice. It had sounded so lovely – perhaps even heavenly – filling my mind, my body, all my senses. But how was that possible?

A framed picture of Jesus stood on the dressing table. Jesus and I locked eyes. Could He have spoken to me? The voice had come from someone, somewhere, and no one else was around.

I could feel the effects of that moment in my body, physically, emotionally. I felt enraptured, bursting with joy. Could it have been Jesus? I'd never heard Him speak before, so how could I know for sure?

I sat on the bed and held the picture of Jesus in my hands. I really needed to keep calm; in fact, I should be sceptical.

I tried to relive the moment. Did the voice question or command? Was it 'Will you make reparation?' or 'Make reparation'. Two words or four? I didn't know. It had happened so fast.

I tried to make sense of it. One thing was certain – I felt elated. Five, ten, fifteen minutes slipped by as I continued to sit and think. Faith versus disbelief. Hope versus despair. It wasn't too difficult to believe in God. Or the voice of God. I knew I hadn't invented it, so I ought to accept it, though I decided not to tell anyone; especially Mother. This was between me and God.

I thought of the sins of my past with shame. I had messed up and abandoned my baby. I had been naïve to think that I could get away with it, minus any emotional consequences. I was finding that idea more impossible to believe, despite what Father John had told me in Melbourne. Surely, there was a price to pay for my sins.

I needed to wash myself clean, to purify myself. Jesus was giving me a message. How could I ignore Him? I resolved to pray more, to try harder – that was my commitment, nothing further.

Pope Gregory was asking everyone to come to Palmar de Troya and join the Carmelites of the Holy Face as priests and nuns, to pray for the salvation of the world. Yet, I knew I didn't have the grace of a religious vocation, sweet as that thought may have been. History had proven that beyond any doubt. Nevertheless, as the months passed, another voice inside my head challenged my resistance, prodding and poking and never letting up.

If Jesus was asking the ultimate sacrifice of me, would He not help me along the way? Would He not give me the strength to live the life of a Carmelite nun? Where was my faith? My love?

On the other hand, if He didn't want me to go to Palmar de Troya, why bother speaking to me? Surely, He had better things to do than waste His time confusing me.

Chapter 18
The Village

There was no big family send-off, no tearful farewells. I said good-bye to my parents, "I'll see you in heaven." To everyone else I pretended I was simply going overseas, visiting the family in Belfast, then on to Spain – and I would return. It was August 1982, barely twelve months since my trip to America.

As I stepped off the plane at San Pablo Airport, the main international airport in Seville situated some nine kilometres east of the city, my heart was exploding with happiness. Outside the terminal, fierce dry heat shimmered with airport fumes. I headed straight for the taxi stand.

"Palmar de Troya? Yes?" I asked the first driver.

He looked surly and shook his head. I walked to the next taxi. Same response. Palmar de Troya wasn't a favourite destination.

After my fourth attempt, a driver took pity on me, muttered something I didn't understand, opened the boot and then left me to manage my suitcase. I settled into the back seat, relieved that the air-conditioning was switched on. As we drove away from San Pablo Airport I felt fantastic – a new life in a foreign land awaited me, a life I had chosen. I was trusting God with my life: past, present and future. I was offering my life to God as a sacrifice; not as a nun chosen by God but as a gift, from me to Him, freely given. I was taking charge, determining my way forward, with confidence. The voice I had heard in my bedroom had empowered me.

The flawless Sevillian sky, painted indigo blue, provided the backdrop for the city skyline, a mix of ancient and modern. Apartment buildings and office towers amidst spires and steeples, bell-towers and minarets, fountains and sculptures dating back to the time of the Moors. To the Baroque and Classical periods. To the voyages of Christopher Columbus, who is buried in the Cathedral of Seville, one of the largest cathedrals in Christendom.

Through the city centre, the waters of the Guadalquivir River flowed effortlessly, spanned by old Roman bridges. Ornamental orange trees bordered the riverbanks, glistening in the sunlight, exuding sweet fragrance. Groves of tall palms swayed exotically in the light breeze. Thousands of multi-coloured potted flowers cascaded cheekily from balconies and windows in high-rise apartment blocks. I loved it all.

Soon we were leaving Seville and motoring into the countryside. But there was no bright green grass, no woolly sheep, no fat cows – nothing to remind me of New Zealand – just dry reddish-brown fields, the ancient floodplains of the Guadalquivir River, stretching endlessly.

We sat in silence, the driver and me, as we passed through two or three deserted towns. I pitied the people whose houses bordered the unscaled road. More empty fields whizzed past, then countless rows of gnarly olive trees, dating back centuries. Thousands of rows, millions of trees, their ugliness belying the rich river of oil buried within the fruit.

Beyond the undulating hills of the olive plantations, atop the highest point, sat the Cathedral of Palmar de Troya. Isolated, superior, symbolic. Revered and loathed. I turned my attention back towards the desolate landscape, noting something of the extent to which the cathedral was completely out of context with the simple peasant life of the locals living in its shadow.

A few minutes later, the driver turned off the highway and drove into the village of Palmar de Troya. He stopped and motioned for me to get out. A huddle of dwellings painted white, tumbling one after the other, lined both sides of the dirt road. The village was poor and humble, no doubt serving the needs of local farmers and little else.

"*Cuantos?*" I asked the taxi driver.

He muttered something I didn't understand. I opened the palm of my hand and he helped himself to the fare. He gave me some change and I hoped he was honest. I also hoped he would pick up another fare on his way back to Seville, making his trip worthwhile.

"*Gracias*," I said as he handed me my suitcase.

"*Gracias a usted, tambien*," he muttered.

A few old women, dressed in black, carried buckets full of water from the well. He slammed the car doors shut, then waved. The dust rose, ballooned and settled again.

August – the middle of summer, scorching hot, and forty degrees. Yapping dogs and gruff male voices punctuated the silence, directing my attention to the other side of the road. Tools and muscles were grinding and scraping behind closed doors.

"*Mañana, por la mañana,*" someone shouted.

"*Si, mañana.*"

"*Adios, amigo.*"

I could taste the sweat pouring down their faces but I couldn't see them. The road was deserted, and every door tightly shut.

A few seconds later a woman appeared, dressed in a long brown cape.

"*¿Usted habla español?*" Do you speak Spanish? She smiled brightly as she walked towards me, her cheeks red, her eyes intensely blue.

"Do you speak English?" I asked, deliberately enunciating each word clearly.

"*Oui, oui,*" she said, tugging at a few strands of grey hair that had slipped out from beneath her brown headscarf.

We both laughed. I hadn't expected to hear French. We exchanged a few words in pidgin English and she directed me to a pilgrim house.

There was a women's house and a men's house. In the women's house I met three more pilgrims who were keen to speak English and curious to know all about me.

"Life in the Order is very tough," one warned.

"Would you like me to tell the Mother General that you want to enter?" the French woman asked.

One of the women came from Vietnam; the other two, a mother and daughter, had emigrated from India to England. I sensed I had nothing in common with them, other than religion. I hoped they weren't fanatical or eccentric but genuinely spiritual and enlightened.

I remembered Jesus' words in St Matthew's Gospel, 11:25: *'I praise you Father, Lord of heaven and earth because you have hidden these things from the wise and learned and revealed them to little children'*. I comforted myself with those words, hoping they were relevant. I was chancing my life on those words, risking it all. The city of Rome, with all its splendour, had been abandoned by God. The true Church was in the catacombs, at Palmar de Troya.

The interior of the pilgrim house was sparsely furnished, the floors tiled, the walls whitewashed. All the bedrooms were piled high with bunks. I had a room to myself because there were very few pilgrims in the village. The pilgrims only arrived in big numbers for the important feast days at Easter and in July and October.

I put my suitcase on one of the spare beds, then walked outside to inspect the village. I wanted to get a sense of its shape and size; to breathe its holy air. I turned corner after corner of dirt roads and closed doors. Everyone was taking a siesta.

On returning to the pilgrim house, the women encouraged me to walk up to the cathedral with them for evening prayers. They said we needed to go together for safety reasons. Several years earlier, a few pilgrims had been mugged by locals who were opposed to Clemente and his group. The opposition and hostility had increased with Clemente's elevation to the Papacy.

I collected a black lace mantilla from my room before joining the women downstairs. They were dressed in flat shoes, shapeless long brown capes and brown headscarves. I was in a black and blue circular skirt, mid-calf, with a white blouse nipped in at the waist by a metallic belt, chunky bangles on one wrist, and long hair hanging down my back. Even ignoring the high-heeled, strappy sandals, my clothes alone told everyone that this was my first visit to Palmar de Troya – and that I was still a fashion-conscious young woman, despite my religion.

"Flat shoes would be better," someone said. But I didn't have any with me.

We walked along the main street and around a corner. The village of Palmar de Troya tucked neatly into the natural contour of the landscape at the base of the hillside. It was easy to sympathise with the villagers who objected to what they saw as a monstrosity on top of their hill, dwarfing the village. The cathedral was bold, resolute and austere. Gothic in style, with bell towers and cupolas, it looked more like a fortress than a house of God.

Children from the village had played on the hillside for centuries, guarding herds of goats, picking flowers, and hunting for little treasures like insects and pebbles. But that world had changed forever, one day in 1968, when four children came home late for dinner, saying that the

Blessed Virgin Mary had appeared to them and wanted them to pray the Rosary.

Each evening, at 5:30 pm, we climbed the hill to the cathedral compound which was protected by a solid six-metre-high wall, iron gates, armed security guards and dogs. Someone knocked on the gate and we waited for the guard to open the viewing shutter to check our identity.

"Queremos entrar, por favour." We want to come in, please.

The French woman always spoke first.

"Si, si," the guard replied.

The iron door clanged as he slid the shutter closed. There was more banging as he withdrew the bolts and opened the doorway. As my feet stepped over the threshold, I felt my heart thumping.

"Si, si," he repeated, as he checked our clothing.

Entry to the compound was granted only to those pilgrims correctly dressed according to the Palmarian dress code, which mirrored what had traditionally been enforced at the Vatican in Rome. For men: long trousers, long-sleeved shirts buttoned at the neck, socks and shoes. For women: skirts or dresses to at least mid-calf, with long sleeves, stockings and shoes, and a mantilla or scarf covering the head. Tight and see-through material was definitely not permitted. Many pilgrims, copying the nuns, wore brown from head to toe, some covering themselves in full-length brown capes.

I adjusted the scapular I was wearing over my clothing. It was an important part of the dress code. Legend says that St Simon Stock, a fourteenth-century English monk, received a vision of Mary handing him the scapular and promising eternal salvation for the wearer. Popes throughout the centuries had reiterated the benefits and graces of wearing the scapular. Pope Gregory had made it compulsory.

Traditionally, the scapular consisted of a short length of brown cord worn around the neck, with two small holy pictures hanging down back and front. It was always worn under the clothing. Pope Gregory's scapular was larger and worn on top, with red ribbons and pictures of the face of Christ, similar to that of the Shroud of Turin.

The cathedral was a huge empty shell, still very much a construction site, with towers of scaffolding reaching high up to the vaulted ceiling. The main altar was beautifully carved out of dark pink marble, and adorned by a statue of Mary elaborately dressed in material, Spanish style.

Statues of famous saints decorated side altars. Saint Christopher, whom the Roman Catholic Church had recently demoted but the Palmarian Church had reinstated, was holding the baby Jesus on his shoulders, ready to carry him over the river. Saint Anthony, my favourite saint, wore his traditional brown robe and white lily, his head clearly tonsured. Saint Anne, the mother of Mary, and Saint Thérèse of Lisieux, the little flower, were equally recognisable. Likewise, Saint Teresa of Avila, the great Spanish mystic whose incorrupt hand had lain on President Franco's desk throughout his presidency.

A short, fat nun approached me. She was on door-duty, vetting all the women. A priest was standing guard on the other side of the entrance, vetting the men. Women and men were segregated in church: women on the right, men on the left.

The nun wore a long black veil covering her head and face, with a traditional, full-length Carmelite habit. She looked peculiar because she was faceless. Even her hands were hidden from sight, being tucked neatly beneath a length of cream material, also called a scapular, which hung over her long brown robe.

She took a minute or two to scrutinize me, even checking my toes to make sure I was wearing pantyhose. I thought the dress code was extreme, and the efforts taken to enforce compliance even more excessive. But I reminded myself that I was a sinner, and that humility and modesty were required of me.

"*Si, si, venga, por favor.*" She told me to come forward as she shuffled back to her kneeler.

I walked halfway down the nave of the church before kneeling on the cold concrete floor. There were no pews and the cathedral was almost empty. The congregation of fifteen to twenty laypeople was laughable or, should I say, pitiful.

Was this a joke? Was this the new Rome? Was God truly raising up the lowly and confounding the wise? My stomach tightened in knots.

A group of fifty nuns knelt at the front on the right hand side, the women's side. They looked identical, buried beneath layers of black and brown material. The black veils over their faces created a private cloister for each of them. I imagined myself kneeling with them, hidden behind a veil, my secret safe – between me and God. My intentions were noble, my heart willing, my soul ready: ready for chastisement, for purification.

The pantomime continued to unfold. A dozen or more priests, dressed in long black soutanes with flaming red sashes and skull caps, gathered at the side altars where they vested for Mass in beautiful vibrant colours. They were cardinals, Princes of the Church. Some looked impressive, standing straight and tall. I searched their faces – the old, the young, the pure, the wise, the proud, the tested and the venerable. Two or three were mere boys.

Throughout centuries of Christianity, men have enjoyed a special role in the Catholic Church. Only they are elevated to the priesthood. Only they can perform the sacraments. Only they have the power to forgive sins, to remove the stain of Original Sin, or change a Communion wafer into the Body and Blood of Jesus.

Women have always played a lesser role in the Catholic Church and, at Palmar de Troya, the age-old disparity between men and women was even more evident. The nuns were invisible while the priests were dressed in spectacular costumes on a religious stage: the altar of God.

I knew where I wanted to be – with the nuns, on my knees, praying for peace and salvation for the entire world. I felt excited because I had a purpose. It seemed like a mighty purpose.

Every night four religious services took place, each service lasting one and a half to two hours. Mass was combined with the Penitential Rosary, the Way of the Cross, and The Trisagio – a prayer to the Holy Trinity. Exposition of the Blessed Sacrament, with an outdoor procession, and Benediction were part of the usual timetable. Ten-minute breaks between the services allowed everyone to stretch their legs outside or to use the bathroom. Laypeople left through the main doors at the rear while priests and nuns exited through side doors at the front: priests on the left, nuns on the right, thus preventing any communication. The clangour of bells tolling in the soaring towers summoned everyone inside for the next service.

We hurried back to the village at the end of prayers each night, struggling to keep pace with the laymen who had torches. There were no street lamps and the women seemed nervous.

At 6:00 pm on Saturday night, the bells tolled to start the all-night vigil of prayer, calling pilgrims, and reminding villagers – whether they liked it or not. Every couple of hours, throughout the night, they tolled again to start the next service.

I wandered back to the village at about 2:00 am with some of the other pilgrims. By that time of night we were utterly exhausted.

"The nuns and priests will pray until the vigil ends at about 8 am," someone said.

I had no idea how I was going to stay awake every Saturday night when I was a nun. In the meantime, though, I intended to sleep.

A couple of weeks later, busloads of pilgrims disembarked in the village, and all the cardinals who were stationed overseas returned to Seville. They stayed at the Pope's residence in the city and attended the ceremonies at the cathedral each night.

On October 12, the feast day of Our Lady of the Pillar, Patron Virgin of Spain, the cathedral was packed before 6:00 pm. Pope Gregory appeared, seated on the *sedia gestatoria* and carried high in the air by twelve cardinals. The crowd of believers went wild with excitement.

Cries of *"Viva Su Santidad El Papa Gregorio Diez y Siete,"* (Long live Pope Gregory XVII) pierced the air and echoed in the vaulted ceiling. The congregation responded with a thunderous, *"Viva!"* as the euphoria intensified.

As he came closer to where I was standing, I noted many details, especially his composure. When he stood up to bless the congregation, everyone gasped. The atmosphere was electric. He looked short and stout, and was dressed in a white soutane with matching cape. A three-tiered papal crown rested proudly on his head, almost hiding his jet black hair, neatly trimmed. His eye sockets were empty, eyelids wrinkled and sunken. He truly was blind.

The procession completed its circle, the congregation hushed, the *sedia gestatoria* lowered, and Pope Gregory was assisted down. He strode into the sanctuary where he stopped at the altar steps, aided by two cardinals, one on either side.

"*In nomine Patris et Filii et Spiritus Sancti. Amen.*" In the name of the Father and of the Son and of the Holy Spirit. Amen. His voice was deep and thunderous.

For the next two days and nights, incense filled the air as everyone prayed in Latin. The following morning the pilgrims departed, and village life returned to normal, to quietness and simplicity of daily routines. And I was, once again, enveloped in its desert cloak – winding down, losing myself in obscurity, as I retreated further from reality in preparation for entering the Order of the Carmelite nuns.

Chapter 19
The Carmelite Nuns

One night the nun on door-duty told me that the Mother General would speak to me in the next ten-minute break. That was the news I was wanting to hear.

After Benediction that night I stood on the cathedral steps as instructed. A few minutes later the Mother General appeared, accompanied by another nun. They were both tall, their faces well hidden beneath black veils. She greeted me warmly in a thick Irish brogue.

"I visited my family in Belfast before coming to Seville," I said. I thought she would like to hear that.

"Belfarst! Tharr all lunatics up there," she said.

Oops!

"All the Irish girls in the Order are from the South."

"My great great uncle was a famous Irish artist—"

"The Irish girls are magnificent. Some of them are saints. There are t'ree siblings from one Irish family, and five siblings from a Spanish family – all in the Order."

"I was a music teacher in—"

"What ya did in the world is irrelevant," she said, threading her thumbs through the cord at her waist in a very unfeminine pose. "When ya enter the Order, ya start at the bottom."

The cathedral bells rang and they went inside. The ten-minute break was ridiculously short for an interview.

The following night, during another break, she walked through the cathedral and motioned for me to follow her outside. As we conversed on the steps, she seemed more relaxed than the previous day, even allowing the English nun who was with her to ask some questions.

We had several more meetings on the steps before she said the Pope had given permission for me to enter the Order.

"The Porpe has given ya the name *Paloma*, which is 'dove' in Spanish," she said. "Ya religious name will be *Hermana Maria Paloma,* which means Sister Maria Paloma. Everyone in the Order includes 'Maria' as part of their name."

"Sounds lovely."

"The dove has special significance in scripture, ya know. Noah released a dove to determine if the flood waters had subsided. And, of course, the dove represents the Hoorly Spirit. It is a sign of peace and purity."

Peace and purity… Very appropriate, I thought. The prayer of Saint Francis of Assisi was my mantra. I fell asleep every night asking God to make me an instrument of His peace. And purity, that elusive grace that had caused me so much frustration, was now associated with my new name. But would I live up to it?

The rest of the week disappeared in a blur as I counted down to Saturday night – the night I was entering the Order of the Carmelites of the Holy

Face of Jesus. By 2:45 am I was tired and hungry. My knees felt stiff and sore – the concrete floor, cold and hard. All sense of time had vanished. The shapeless forms of the nuns were making their way to the rear of the cathedral and disappearing through a doorway.

Two nuns walked over to where I was kneeling.

"Maria?"

"Yes," I replied.

"Mother General said to tell ya to follow us doon to the crypt. We're goin' to have our supper dah in a minute."

I stood up and followed them through the doorway. A spiral staircase led us underground. It was cold, dark and unlit. I held onto the handrail to steady myself. Step by step my feet took me deeper – the descent into darkness symbolizing the death of my old self, my need to leave behind the weakness of my flesh and live entirely for Christ. I paused, overwhelmed, feeling lost and abandoned.

At the bottom of the staircase, a shaft of light led us into a big room where all the nuns had gathered. They had tossed off their black veils so I could see their smiling faces. They were a strange mix of cultures and age groups: young and old, short and fat, tall and lean. With blue eyes and brown eyes, ivory skin and rosy cheeks, dimples and freckles and lots of wrinkles, they came from Britain, Europe, North and South America, Africa, and India.

They stood in silence on either side of simple trestle tables covered in plastic tablecloths, their brown and black habits contrasting with the stark white walls and unpainted concrete floor. I was motioned to go to the table at the far end of the room.

The roll was called and each nun answered "*Viva la Santa Faz*" Long live the Holy Face. At the end of the roll call I heard my name called out for the first time: *Hermana Maria Paloma*. And I replied, "*Viva la Santa Faz.*"

We ate in silence, the meal consisting of cold scrambled eggs, dry bread and water. At the end of the meal the dishes were washed and dried. Then the nuns returned to the cathedral to pray until morning. I joined them. The all-night vigil of prayer finally finished at 7:45 am on Sunday morning.

We returned to Seville in a convoy of vans driven by *los padres* (the priests). The driver and his companion sat in the front with the nuns seated behind in rows of threes and fours. Four other nuns were crammed into the back with me. The ride was bumpy and our folding seats slid around on the metal floor. We couldn't see anything because there were no windows in the back. The journey took about forty-five minutes and the nuns prayed loudly the entire journey. The noise was awful.

During the next three days I stayed *en casa*, at home, in silence and confined to a bedroom, praying and reading my Bible. The Superior said there had been a medical emergency overnight and, therefore, all plans were on hold. The house was very quiet and dark. I was allowed to join the community for morning Mass and meals but nothing else.

On the third day the Mother General arrived at the abbey to clothe me in a second-hand habit, assisted by her companion. They chatted easily in lilting Irish accents – the rule of silence momentarily suspended.

We were in a storage room, cluttered with boxes and a screen. The Mother General slumped into the only chair. I stepped behind the screen to undress.

The habit was full of patches, with a false hem. The underdress was made of brown and white gingham, and the overdress was in heavy brown serge. Both tunics were long and baggy, and pleated at the neck. A waistband and pockets held the underdress in place, while a knotted cream cord belted the brown serge. It had slits in the side seams to access the pockets underneath.

"That looks like it fits all right," the Mother General said, her dimples accentuated by the rosiness of her cheeks, and her blue eyes twinkling with kindness.

"Now, try this on," the assistant said, handing me a white head covering.

I slipped it over my head so that only my face was visible in the opening. It was so tight it strangled me around the jaw.

"Och, dorn't worry," the Mother General said. "We'll get ya another one in a few deys."

They both laughed.

Eating was going to be impossible.

"These are the only black sandals we harve," the assistant said.

I tried them on but they were much too small.

"You'll have to wear them, Hermana Maria Paloma," the Mother General said. "We'll give ya another pair when the pilgrims bring more, but we have no idea when that will be."

At least the long black socks fitted.

A length of cream material, representing the scapular of Our Lady of Mount Carmel, was placed over my head, hanging down front and back over the tunic. A maroon veil was put on my head, and attached by a strip of Velcro. The veil hung down to my waist.

It would have been nice to see what I looked like but mirrors were not allowed. I asked about the significance and history of the various parts of the habit.

"The habit was given to Porpe Gregory by Our Blessed Lord Himself," the Mother General said. "That's all that matters. That's all ya need to know."

The tone of her voice stopped me asking any more questions. She had missed an opportunity to educate me in the rich and wonderful history of monastic life. I thought of Saint Francis of Assisi and Saint Clare. I was sure that every article of clothing must have special significance. I decided to find a book and read about it as soon as possible.

The old habit was for working in during the day, she said. I would be given another one in better condition to wear to the cathedral each afternoon.

"The habit is a sign of poverty and membership in the Order."

I certainly felt poor.

The assistant tied a black veil on top of the maroon veil, hiding the one underneath.

I felt lost beneath the layers of clothing.

"The final piece," she said, flinging a sheer black veil over my head and face.

We all laughed. I could hardly see.

"Now ya look like a Carmelite nun, Hermana Maria Paloma," the Mother General said.

"You can cut your hair if you like, but, remember, not too short. In twelve months' time you will take ya first vows and ya head will be uncovered for that ceremony."

"Okay."

"The top veil is used at the cathedral, and in the abbey during Mass," the assistant said. "The rest of the time it's folded over the cream cord around your waist."

She flicked it off my head and folded it neatly for me, showing me how to thread it over the cord. It was very bulky. Then she held up a long brown cape and an old, white, cotton nightdress to try for size. I packed them into my suitcase, together with another head covering for bed, some spare socks, and long white pants and singlets, before closing the lid.

"Are ya ready, Hermana Maria Paloma? "

"Yes, Mother General."

We walked along several dark passageways to the front door where the Superior was waiting. They spoke in Spanish for a few minutes. Then the Superior opened the door and I stepped outside, accompanied by two other nuns.

I was, officially, a member of the Carmelites of the Holy Face of Jesus, *in* the world but not *of* the world. I belonged. During the previous eight years all my efforts to connect with something or someone had been thwarted. Now, at last, I had arrived. And, what was more, I could bury my secret even deeper, beneath layers of Carmelite clothing, protected by a rule of silence and a desire to repent. No one in the Order knew anything about me and I was never going to tell them. The past was the past – buried forever.

We walked around the corner in silence. A street name, *Abad Gordillo,* followed by another street, *Calle Alfaqueque.* We were in the very heart of the 'old quarter' of Seville, on the east bank of the Guadalquivir River.

Terraced housing in the cobblestoned lane was three or four storeys high, and painted in drab, muted colours. Front doors opened directly onto the cobblestones. There was no car access. Street-level windows were covered with iron bars and shutters, designed to keep out heat, dust and burglars. The overall impression was one of neglect.

I promised myself that I would do my best. I would pour my heart and soul into every aspect of my new life, selflessly and lovingly.

Fifty metres down the road we stopped outside another abbey that was to be my new home. The front door opened and we stepped inside.

"Ave Maria purissima." Hail Mary most pure, I said, copying the two nuns who had entered before me.

"Sin pecado concebido." Conceived without sin, replied the nun who had opened the door. A black veil hid her face.

This greeting was always used on arriving and leaving the abbey. The words come from the Gospel of St Luke, when the Archangel Gabriel appeared to Mary saying She would conceive a Son.

My companions left, without another word. The Superior locked and bolted the heavy wooden door behind them. She lifted her black veil off her face, smiled, and moved towards a wrought iron gate at the far end of the front entrance.

"Come this way, Hermana Maria Paloma." She was Japanese with a soft American accent, and she glided over the floor without making a sound. She seemed nice.

I followed her through to the internal ground floor courtyard which was dark and cool. Four storeys above, a glass roof protected the courtyard in all weathers. As we climbed the narrow staircase, I realised that each successive floor was built around the courtyard which provided the only natural light in the abbey. All external windows at the front of the building were covered by wooden blinds and shutters, and there were no windows on the other sides of the house.

The floors were tiled, as were the walls – to chest height. The influence of the Arab culture, with its complex geometric patterns in vibrant colours, hinted at a very different lifestyle from the one lived by the nuns. Cobalt blues and greens, with pinks and reds associated with the

Mediterranean coast, combined with sunflower yellows, set against white backgrounds. Above the tiles, the bare walls were plastered and painted white.

At each floor I glimpsed another inquisitive face peering out of layers of Carmelite clothing. Everyone looked happy and welcoming.

My room was on the rooftop, the fourth floor. It wasn't much bigger than a shoebox – barely one and a half metres by two metres. The bed was made of unpainted wood with a simple frame, a piece of chipboard, and a foam mattress ten centimetres thick. There were sheets, a blanket and a pillow. Plaster flaked off the walls in a few places, and tiles wobbled under my feet.

"Put your veil over your face if you want to look out the window," the Superior said.

What could I possibly see with a veil over my face? It seemed like a strange thing to do.

The window opened out to a ventilation shaft connected to the adjoining building a few metres away – too close for comfort. All the rooftops in the street were connected. Who were our neighbours? Were we in a safe part of the city?

I tried to close the shutters but they didn't fit, nor did the window frame. The room was so poor it felt like a prison cell in a Third World country.

"Put your suitcase on the floor in that corner," she said, trying to be helpful.

We exchanged smiles. There was hardly room for a person, let alone a suitcase.

"You'll find a plastic bucket to wash in under the bed. There's very little hot water in the abbey so everyone washes in their room."

I peered at the old bucket, wondering if I would ever feel clean again.

She looked at her watch. "It's nearly time for the bell. Spiritual Reading is at 1:30 pm. You can read in your room but most nuns prefer to read in the chapel – less chance of falling asleep."

"Okay."

"This is the Book of Rules," she said, handing me a small booklet. "It was dictated to Pope Gregory by God Himself. You could read it today in Spiritual Reading."

"Thank you."

"Although The Rule forbids any unnecessary talking, Spanish is the only language we use for communication. However, you're allowed to speak English for now, if you need to talk. The Mother General says common sense must prevail."

"That's good."

"Lunch is at 2:00 pm. You've just got time to organise your room."

My room! An empty cell, except for a bed and an unpainted wooden box.

I put the nightie and head covering under the pillow, and hung the long brown cape on a nail behind the bright green door. My Bible and alarm clock went on the box at the top of the bed.

The sound of the bell rose from the courtyard below – twelve even chimes. I closed the bedroom door and looked over the balustrade. Nuns were hurrying from all directions.

"Rapido!" someone whispered.

"Shh."

"Silencio."

I joined the procession on the stairs. Old nuns, riddled with arthritis, were clinging to the handrail. The young were impatient, squeezing past them.

"Rapido!"

Three more chimes rang out. Everyone was standing in a semi-circle in the courtyard, hands neatly hidden behind cream scapulars. The Superior arrived and another three chimes were sounded: my first roll call, dressed as a Carmelite. After Spiritual Reading the bell rang again for another roll call, this time on the third floor landing outside the refectory.

Lunch was a three course meal: thick soup and dry bread, with a small measure of cheap red wine, followed by sardines, omelette and salad, then fresh fruit. The Vice-Superior ladled the first course, and then served the second, onto the very same plates.

A tiny old nun was pleading, pointing at the mountain of food on her plate. *"Madre Superiora, por caridad."* Mother Superior, please.

"Silencio," the Superior said, shaking her head. She pinched her lips tight and lowered her eyes.

There were eleven of us crowded into the refectory. It was a very tight fit and several nuns were frowning. Someone muttered in German. Either she didn't like sardines or she had been served too much food too.

"Obediencia," the Superior said through clenched teeth.

My stomach was churning. I hated sardines. I hoped I wouldn't vomit. Sipping soup had been difficult with my jaw locked tight by the head covering, but chewing was going to be impossible. I wondered what God thought, looking down from above.

Chapter 20
The Abbey

Life in the abbey was controlled by the bell which represented the voice of God. The bell rang frequently, from the time to rise at 6:40 am until the time to go to bed, sometime after dinner and dishes, at about 1:30 am the following day.

The Book of Rules was the pathway to holiness and I knew I would have trouble reconciling the one with the other. Silence was compulsory at all times, except during recited prayers, although some nuns took liberties, not only by speaking but by using their native languages.

When I climbed the stairs to my room on that first night I felt tired but optimistic. We had left the abbey at 3:30 pm, walked in procession to another abbey around the corner, travelled in vans through Seville and out to the cathedral for seven hours of prayers, before returning home, eating dinner and, finally, going to bed.

My stomach was bursting from another plate of sardines, omelette and salad. My jaw was aching, my feet swollen. I opened the cell door and peered out into the semi-darkness, listening carefully. Slowly, the noises in the abbey were dying away. I was waiting to use the bathroom on the rooftop.

On the floor below, I saw a nun in her underwear. She was leaning over the balustrade, fanning her face with both hands, begging a breeze to spiral down from the rooftop above. Dressed in a white head covering, her ample bosom and rolls of tummy fat were hidden beneath a singlet, and her bulging thighs were concealed inside long baggy pants to the knee. She was enjoying a quiet moment, alone; the first and only opportunity of a long day and an even longer night. I could relate to that need, even if she was breaking the rules.

If a nun left her room at night, she had to wear a nightie over her underwear, covered by a brown tunic, with a maroon veil over the head covering. Any deliberate breaking of the rules had to be acknowledged in writing to the Superior of the abbey who informed the Mother General, who told Padre Isidoro and, he, the Pope. If we broke the rules, we were forbidden from receiving Holy Communion until the Pope said otherwise, and this information was communicated back down the chain of command.

I tip-toed to the bathroom so the underwear nun wouldn't hear me. Half an hour later I turned off my light. It was difficult to fall asleep: the mattress was thin, the air hot and stuffy.

Next morning at Mass I was surprised to see the underwear nun receive Holy Communion with everyone else. I wondered how many other rules she'd broken when she thought no one was watching.

After breakfast the Superior sent me to my room to embroider my name on my clothing.

"It will probably take you a few days," she said. "Some nuns have taken a whole week to finish the task."

I disliked sewing, but I was fast, so I finished in three hours. A single red stitch, from point to point, was more than adequate in my opinion. No twenty tiny pinpricks in fancy cursive style for me.

The next day the Superior told me to clean the bathrooms, and to sweep and wet mop all the floors, excluding bedrooms, kitchen and chapel. Two elderly nuns were praying the Rosary in the chapel downstairs. It was a dark, empty space at the front of the house. An oil lamp flickered in the corner. White linen cloths, brass candlesticks, a tabernacle and some small statues adorned the altar. There was no pews, only an altar and altar rails. The nuns sat on small canvas folding stools, leaning against the back wall, heads bowed, mumbling softly.

The second floor was full of landings and bedrooms; the third floor, home to the kitchen and refectory. There were two bathrooms in the abbey, one on the second floor, the other on the fourth. On the rooftop, three nuns were busy ironing and praying the Rosary aloud.

There was no lounge, no comfortable chairs, no television or radio, no newspaper or telephone, and no communication with the outside world. Unfortunately, there was no library either, not even a few dusty shelves of tatty books, so I never did discover the significance of the various parts of the habit. And, since we lived in silence, I wasn't allowed to ask.

Two weeks later the Superior told me to go to the kitchen and cook. Immediately after morning Mass, I went upstairs and cut slices of crusty white bread and cheese. The cheeses came in large circular blocks – mostly Dutch Edam or Cheddar but occasionally a scrumptious Spanish Manchego or Roncal. There was no butter or margarine on the dining table, only raw garlic, olive oil and vinegar. I boiled the kettle, the bell rang, followed by the roll call and blessing on the third floor, and we filed into the refectory. Dry bread tasted delicious but I did miss butter those first few days. Fresh fruit eaten with cutlery, no fingers allowed, and a cup of either tea or coffee completed the meal. Officially, the morning's work started at 9:40 am and continued until 1 pm, except for the nun in the kitchen.

A South American nun had been told by the Superior to instruct me on the menu for lunch and dinner. Why didn't the Superior choose someone who spoke English?

"Comprendes, Hermana Maria Paloma?"

I stared at her in mild frustration. Sign language proved more useful.

The kitchen was very small, with just enough room for a wobbly table, gas stove and oven, and a set of shelves covered in old pots and pans, all badly warped. A window opened into the same ventilation shaft as my cell above, except there was no breeze to relieve the heat. A fridge stood on the landing at the kitchen doorway.

Fortunately, the underwear nun poked her head into the kitchen throughout the morning, muttering in German and smiling contentedly. It helped. She wanted to make sure I knew what I was doing.

Although there were no condiments in the kitchen, garlic and onion created a good base for vegetable and bean soups. But what could I do with sardines to make them edible? That was my biggest concern. There were no cook books to give me any inspiration but, at least, I was able to cook the sardines thoroughly so they weren't served half-raw, unlike the efforts of the previous cook.

The priests delivered boxes of food to the front door every week and we ate whatever they delivered. As the young nuns carried the food upstairs, elderly nuns muttered and scowled. *"Demasiado."* Too much. Neither the Mother General nor the Superior seemed able to control the quantity of food that arrived. A dietician had prepared a suitable menu for us and everyone in the Order ate the same food at every meal. My task was to make it taste delicious. I had already decided that our life was difficult enough without mealtime being a further source of penance.

Fifty eggs in an omelette for lunch was normal, whipped by hand. Each day I prepared two hundred sardines or fifty herrings for lunch and dinner. The Vice-Superior was ruthless when she served the food. Everyone received the same amount, irrespective of age or body size. Leftovers were not allowed.

The Superior, accompanied by another nun, spent every morning away from the abbey, on business for the Mother General. In her absence the Vice-Superior, who was Indian, prowled around the abbey, dragging her feet and rustling her habit. Her voice was unusually strident and her flashy smile could sour, quickly, as her face darkened with annoyance. She made me feel uncomfortable. Why had the Mother General chosen her for promotion? Her abrasive personality seemed the antithesis of virtue to me.

Every morning she reminded me to go to the chapel at 11:00 am to recite the Rosary for an hour – as if I was an old nun with a failing memory. Her constant interference resulted in her breaking the silence but her focus was on wielding power, not blissful peace and quiet.

I didn't understand why the Superior thought that one and a half hours were long enough for me to prepare two meals for eleven people; that extra Rosary hour would have been so useful. At least on Saturday I didn't have to go to the chapel, so I had two and a half hours to prepare three meals for eleven people – Saturday's three course lunch, chicken soup for Sunday morning, and roast chicken for Sunday night. I had to gut the chickens; heads, internal organs and feet made good stock. Feet were full of protein and we picked them up in our hands, gnawing them to the bone.

I'd never worked so fast in my life. I motivated myself by comparing my efforts to others in the abbey who seemed to be working even harder than me. If they could do it, so could I. At twenty-eight I was in my prime.

After lunch and washing-up we were allowed a short siesta from 2:45 pm to 3:15 pm. Of course, half an hour wasn't long enough to fall asleep but, at least, we had a chance to lie down, straighten our legs, and try to relax. Adding to the silliness was the need to waste precious time getting semi-undressed because we weren't allowed to lie down in our complete habit.

My mind was a battlefield of questions and criticisms that I would have to find a way to silence. In the meantime, though, I was happy enough, with lots of energy and motivation.

After the siesta we were allowed a cup of tea or coffee before the roll call at 3:30 pm. That one drink had to sustain us until we returned home many hours later. Although we ate an excessive amount of food at mealtimes, my stomach rumbled with hunger pains in between.

From 3:30 pm each afternoon till 9:40 am the following day, silence was broken only by the recitation of formal prayers in unison. Common sense was meant to prevail if there was a problem during the morning's work but, otherwise, all conversation was forbidden.

After being in a stifling kitchen all morning, I looked forward to the trip to the cathedral at 3:30 pm. I loved being outside, feeling the air on my face, the only part of my body that wasn't covered. I looked eagerly along the road, into every porch and window, curious to snatch a glimpse of our neighbours, to get a hint of life on our street. Surprisingly, no one else was in sight, and the whole area seemed deserted; presumably because everyone else was taking a longer siesta than us.

When we reached the next abbey we lined up in the courtyard alongside nuns from five other abbeys – at that time there were seven abbeys with five to twenty nuns in each. Some nuns took out their Rosary beads and started praying silently.

Others lowered their eyes in quiet meditation. My mind usually wandered freely. I was content and relaxed, at the bottom of the Order since I was the newest recruit, with no pressure of expectation, no reputation to protect, and no extra responsibilities. Little did I realise how quickly that would change.

The journey to the cathedral was often terrifying. The nuns prayed the Rosary aloud while the priests fell asleep in the front seats. We could see their heads nodding, their eyelids drooping – micro sleeping – even at the wheel. We weren't allowed to communicate with them so we were at their mercy. Some nuns screamed the prayers, hoping that the noise would wake the driver or earn us God's protection.

Nine hours later we returned to Seville. At that time of night the streets were deserted once again, as everyone was fast asleep. We dragged our feet along the dimly lit cobblestone lane; knees stiff, bodies trembling with exhaustion and hunger. It had been almost twelve hours since lunch.

If anyone had stayed *en casa* that night then our meal was pre-heated, otherwise I ran upstairs to turn on the gas oven and warm the sardines and tortilla. No time was wasted heating up food properly. The salad came out of the fridge, the bread was cut, the bell sounded, the roll call heard, the blessing given on bended knee, and we filed into the refectory.

Bedtime signalled what seemed like the end of a twenty-four hour endurance test. Or the end of a long, hard marathon. Except there were no winners or losers. The important thing was to obey the rules, to do one's work, to stay awake, and to pray aloud. The next day heralded the start of yet another test, day after day, until Saturday night's all-night vigil, when we didn't sleep until after breakfast on Sunday morning. That was a real test of endurance – of one's love, generosity, and commitment.

Unfortunately, at 10:00 am Sunday morning, after enjoying a bowl of chicken soup, and straining to stay awake all night, my body was incapable of sleep. So I lay on my back, wrinkling my swollen toes – the sandals had stretched but were still too tight. Daylight streamed through the shutters that wouldn't close. I focused on the noises in the abbey, slowly fading, then the sounds coming from the street below – voices of people I would never see, and never meet. I stared at the ceiling, the white walls, the green door.

Close your eyes and go to sleep. You're exhausted. Stop thinking.

But there is so much to think about.

I know.

Our life consists of many rules, some of which seem petty and annoying.

Don't be so arrogant. God Himself dictated the Book of Rules to Pope Gregory. You have to humble yourself and obey. That's the process. That will bring holiness.

I guess you're right. Holiness will happen when my thoughts and will have dissolved into God and I no longer exist.

Close your eyes and go to sleep.

If only I could.

Chapter 21
A Personal Attack

Each morning after breakfast we waited for the Superior to dismiss us. If she had any announcements to make, this was the time to deliver them. I knew the routine but I was unprepared for what followed.

"Hermana Maria Paloma, move house," she said.

"Me, *Madre Superiora?"* I asked.

"Si," she said, smiling.

I wondered why she was being so nice but I hid my delight. My initial impression of her had changed dramatically. I had heard her snap once too often.

"Go to the kitchen and cook as usual. And don't forget to leave the kitchen clean."

Some nuns nodded enthusiastically at me. That seemed encouraging.

"There's no time for you to say a Rosary today. Clean your room at one o'clock, pack your bag, change into your good habit, and then you can move next door at 1:30. *¿Comprendes?"*

"Si, Madre Superiora." I was getting used to hearing short sharp instructions, and to answering *'si'* without thinking.

I didn't know there was an abbey next door because I'd never seen any other nuns in the street. Also, I'd never heard any noise next door – no bells tolling, no praying or singing. Since I was sure our neighbours could hear us, I assumed we could hear them, too, but evidently not so.

I wished that someone had told me earlier that there was an abbey next door as it would have allayed my fears at night. I was frightened at night, even though I couldn't remember ever having been scared before by the dark. The sight of metal bars on every window suggested there was a reason for them: to keep intruders out. Not only did my bedroom window not have any bars, it wouldn't close or lock, and it was uncomfortably close to the house next door. I was living in a foreign country where everything was unfamiliar, even the sounds at night.

Cooking was never so easy as on that day. My eyes didn't stream as much from dicing onions, and I didn't notice the burns on my fingers. I'd always been a bit clumsy and still was. However, the news that I was moving felt more like I was escaping – and that was a surprise to me.

Over the previous few weeks I had heard one particular word mentioned with great effect: *el castigo*, punishment. Too many times we had gathered in the gloomy courtyard, waiting for the roll call. There was a little discussion, in German and Spanish. Eyes rolled.

"No Palmar," the Superior snarled.

A tiny German nun answered back. She was old, cantankerous and unyielding.

"Silencio," the Superior commanded.

The underwear nun joined in, with a cheeky smirk.

"No Palmar, para ti, tambien." No Palmar for you, too, the Superior spat.

The Superior had the power to stop them from going to the cathedral. It was the only opportunity in the day to get out of the abbey and go for a drive along *El Paseo de las Delicias* with its fountains and sculptures, palm trees and river banks, royal palace and gardens. Then onto the highway, through shanty towns and barren fields, to the village of Palmar de Troya. And, finally, the cathedral. It was the only opportunity to get away from the Superior and the Vice-Superior because we could kneel wherever we liked at the cathedral. And, since our veils were lowered, we were in a private cloister with God. Nobody was in our face, checking, correcting, or punishing.

I wondered what their lives had been like in Germany. Had they supported Hitler during World War II? Or had they gone into hiding? Had they witnessed horrendous atrocities? Endured heartache and pain? Were they nuns back then? They were certainly old enough to have been. Had their convents been closed or bombed?

My father had fought in that war and my mother's first husband had been shot down and killed. I wanted to know every story of those German nuns, and their faces suggested there was so much to tell. But they weren't allowed to talk and nor was I. Whatever their stories, whether they were allies or enemies, it was irrelevant.

"Las Hostias... problema, Madre Superiora," the tiny nun pleaded.

She'd had to make Holy Communion wafers at another abbey for the past three nights. She was the expert and, although she was too old to work, she was still needed when there were problems with the host-making machine. She was tired and thought she had earned a visit to the cathedral but the Superior needed her to stay and accompany her on some business in the city. There were nine other nuns in the abbey, all willing to accompany the Superior, but the Superior wouldn't budge.

At 1:30 pm that day, I moved to the abbey next door. My new Superior, an elderly German nun, had a heart condition so she had permission from the Mother General to spend every night, except Sunday, at home, praying and resting.

She commanded very little respect from the younger nuns in her abbey. It was easy for them to challenge her. Their energy and strength versus her weakness and poor health; their fluent Spanish versus her pidgin Spanish. She hadn't made any real effort to improve her language skills despite Pope Gregory insisting that Spanish was the most important language on earth and that we must make every effort to learn it.

Three nuns in particular were in a constant power struggle with her during prayers. Even though The Rule stated that prayers must be recited in unison, it followed that the Superior should set the pace. The Superior prayed slowly and deliberately, painfully so, while the young nuns were determined to set a faster pace through sheer volume.

The Mother General led the prayers in the cathedral at a maniacal pace, insisting that the Pope wanted them recited that way. The young nuns took their lead from her, thus justifying the apparent disobedience.

Each morning I knelt in the chapel listening to the pandemonium and feeling embarrassed. The piety and devotion of the Superior was openly challenged by the exuberance and cheek of the younger generation. She suffered the humiliation of being ignored by them, her authority usurped. Neither side was willing to back down, not even for charity's sake, and this surprised me. Fortunately, the ringleader was moved shortly afterwards and the tension during prayers vanished accordingly.

My new bedroom was situated on the ground floor, across the courtyard from the chapel. It was a large dingy room with a high ceiling and one small window fitted with shutters, presumably facing the same ventilation shaft as my previous bedroom. But the window in my new room was so high that I couldn't reach it – so it stayed in a semi-open position all the time. The only furniture in the room was a wooden bed, tucked into one corner.

Winter was approaching and I shivered in bed every night, in foetal position, finding it impossible to sleep in the cold – no money was wasted on heaters. I only had one blanket, which wasn't sufficient, but, as with the sandals a few weeks earlier, the Mother General said she was waiting for the pilgrims to bring some more, whenever that might be. I tried to accept the hardship and not bemoan the lack of organisation.

Christmas arrived but the pilgrims stayed away so the cathedral remained empty. We stayed at the cathedral for three days and nights. None of the rules were relaxed or changed. There were no presents, no talking, and no communication of any kind.

Christmas dinner was special: tinned ham and omelette, followed by lots of mouth-watering sweets and pastries. Everyone smiled contentedly, quietly thinking of home. New Zealand seemed very far away.

"Feliz navidad," (Happy Christmas) the Mother General said warmly at the end of dinner.

"Feliz navidad," everyone replied, but me.

This was my first Christmas in the Order and I was watching what was going on. Suddenly I remembered the pop song 'Feliz Navidad' by José Feliciano, and I started singing it in my head.

"Hermana Maria Paloma! Sing 'Oh Holy Night'," the Mother General commanded in a booming voice.

It was 4:00 am. I stood up and sang as requested. Everyone clapped.

"Silencio, Madres," the Mother General said.

Christmas celebrations were finished. We said a prayer, cleared the tables, and washed the dishes. Some nuns returned to the cathedral to continue the all-night vigil. Each abbey took a turn to lead the Rosary for an hour. The best turns were first or last but the Mother General made sure the timetable was rotated fairly so that everyone got a chance to sleep, although there weren't any beds. The elderly slouched in some shabby armchairs, the young sat outside under the stars on folding chairs, bracing themselves against the chilly winter's night. I didn't have a folding chair so I sat on a concrete ledge, huddled in my long brown cape, identifying with Jesus in the manger at Bethlehem, until the cathedral bells tolled at 7:00 am.

As soon as the Christmas services were finished we returned to the daily routine of life in Seville. A few days later I was given the job of leading the singing at the cathedral. I was meant to keep all the nuns in tune, simply by singing louder than everyone else. But I couldn't – my softer contralto voice was no match for their screaming sirens and booming foghorns. It was very frustrating. I tried to talk to the Mother General but she didn't understand because she was tone deaf.

"Harve more faith, Hermana Maria Paloma," she said.

"Si, Madre," I replied. But I knew it had nothing to do with that.

Two weeks later we were gathered in the courtyard, once again, and the Vice-Superior was translating for the Superior.

"Hermana Maria Paloma, accompany Madre Maria Betania and Madre Maria Caridad to the abbey around the corner, please. The Mother General wants to talk to all the English-speaking nuns."

We looked blankly at each other and shrugged our shoulders. No one knew what was going on and we weren't allowed to ask.

"Si Madre," I replied. "When? Now?"

"Si."

We went to our rooms and changed into our good habits before meeting at the front door. The Superior gave us her blessing, opened the door, and we stepped outside.

The other nuns started talking as soon as the door locked behind us. They could always justify talking, especially in English, and usually targeted me on the way to the kitchen each day. They were kind and well-meaning; one a sensible old lady who delighted in sharing stories about the early days in the Order, the other riddled with arthritis and tormented by horrible voices in her head. I listened with respect.

The three of us had a half-hour Spanish lesson twice a week, although they usually sabotaged the class by talking in English about their own personal problems. One was heavily medicated and needed comforting, the other had a son in the Order and liked to reminisce. I hadn't made much progress in learning Spanish but no one seemed too concerned. I could pray in Spanish and that was the important thing.

As we walked along the road, Madre Maria Betania grabbed my arm to steady herself on the uneven cobblestones. I breathed in the cold winter's air. This was the first time in many weeks that I had felt so free. I was outside, away from the Superior, away from the timetable and the chores.

We turned the corner, then knocked and waited. The door opened and the nun on door-duty told us to go into the dining room and wait in silence for the Mother General. Twelve elderly English-speaking nuns were already seated; some were in their nineties. It was an impressive group and I felt privileged to be there. I was hoping the Mother General had gathered us together for spiritual instruction because, as yet, I hadn't had any formal instruction from anyone.

The Mother General entered and took her place at the head of the table. We all stood and turned to face her, smiling cheerfully. She led a prayer in Spanish: one 'Our Father', one 'Hail Mary' and one 'Glory be'. We sat down, in silence.

"Madres! Hermana Maria Paloma is sitting here tedey with us and brazenly breaking the rules," the Mother General said.

This was no special instruction class for beginners.

"She speaks English all the time."

We locked eyes. Her cheeks were bright red as usual. But her blue eyes – normally twinkling with delight – were icy cold.

"She refuses to speak Spanish. She worn't even try."

I looked away.

You speak to me, in English, all the time at the cathedral. You tell me personal details about the Superiors, about their foibles and personalities, even though I'm last in the Order. English tumbles out of your mouth like a raging waterfall, yet you accuse me.

"Her pride is so greet she t'inks that she'd be humiliatin' herself if she tried to speak Spanish."

She had everyone's attention now, especially mine.

"You see, she doesn't want to appear stupid."

Is that so unreasonable? Show me someone who does.

"She doesn't want to stumble over her words and look like a fool. All the rest of us harve, as we struggled to speak Spanish. But not Hermana Maria Paloma. Ooh no! She's given herself permission to speak English whenever she wants to. She's made up her own rules."

What? Everyone takes liberties with the rules.

"Look at her!" she roared. "Her pride is so greet she's hidin' behind Madre Maria Salvadora."

It was true. I was. I wanted the floor to open up and devour me, although I had done nothing wrong. So who was telling tales? And why? And why was the Mother General changing her own interpretation of the rules? And being so vicious in the process? Where was her charity?

She continued shouting, mocking and abusing me. Unchallenged by anyone in the room, she wound herself into quite a frenzy. Answering back wasn't an option for me or anyone else. When the Mother General spoke, we had to listen. I hung my head in a gesture of humility and resolved never to lift it again.

When we left, twenty minutes later, the two old nuns apologised to me as we walked back to our abbey. But it didn't help.

The Mother General had a nasty side. I had seen it once before. Although we prayed with intensity and fervour as if the salvation of the world depended on us, only two weeks earlier she had punished us by demanding that we pray with *brazos en cruz;* that is, with our arms extended like Jesus on the cross. Most of us prayed in that pose some of the time, raising and lowering our arms as our energy levels came and went. But, now, it was compulsory during all the prayers – in the abbey and at the cathedral.

We were God's army, doing battle with the powers of evil by means of our prayer and penance. Our noble cause lit a fire inside, and that flame had to burn at all times. We were high on adrenalin, riding waves of exhilaration and exhaustion.

Hour upon hour, night after night, I extended my arms like all the other nuns: obediently, generously, silently. After a while my arms ached and I clenched my teeth. But I didn't even know why we were being punished. No one had bothered to tell me.

And, now, this…

I had two options: to stay and put up with the shame and hurt *or* leave. No one would miss me if I left and my leaving would prove that I wasn't prepared to suffer. Nothing more. On the other hand, I wasn't ready to forgive her for what I considered an unjust and abusive attack – even though I knew she had handed me a perfect opportunity to identify with Jesus and make reparation.

Chapter 22
Pomp and Pageantry

The winter's cold was short-lived, only three months, which equated to three months of little or no sleep but plenty of time to think. No extra blankets had arrived with the pilgrims.

More vans had been purchased and I no longer sat in the back, without any windows. I saw road signs for the first time: *Dos Hermanas. Cadiz. Jerez de la Frontera. Utrera.* Such peculiar-looking words. I tried to imagine how to pronounce them as we prayed aloud.

Every day a thin, tired shepherd in a weather-beaten leather hat drove his herd of scrawny goats off the highway and into a paddock. Where was he taking them? There was no grass anywhere.

Further down the highway a lone farmer tilled the drought-stricken soil as he walked behind a pair of bony oxen. I thought of the rolling, green pastures of New Zealand, of flocks of woolly sheep and herds of cows.

There was never much traffic on the highway; mostly tourists in rusty old VW vans. I read the stickers on their rear windows. Unexpected things triggered distant memories, linking me to my past. I was probably the only nun in the Order who could appreciate many of the slogans, advertising Aussie beer, Kiwi culture and being Down Under. With surfboards piled high on roof-racks and scraggly blond hair in the front seat, the colours of the Pacific Ocean came to mind. I wondered what *we* looked like from *their* front seats. A dozen vans filled with nuns, lips moving vigorously, faces peeking out of traditional black veils and white headgear. They were probably telling nun jokes. It made me feel a little better.

Easter arrived and we stayed at the cathedral for the nine days and nights of *Semana Santa* (Holy Week). The cathedral filled to capacity as a thousand pilgrims poured in from all over the world, joined by the Pope and the missionary priests.

In keeping with Spanish tradition, elaborate outdoor processions of religious floats were held every night in the compound. Hidden beneath our black veils and brown capes, we led the procession in double file, carrying lanterns. I recalled the parable of the ten virgins. The wise ones had enough oil to keep their wicks lit. They were ready to meet their bridegroom. Was I ready to meet Jesus? First vows were only six months away if I was going to stay in the Order.

The pilgrims followed behind us, also in double file. Then came the cardinals, dressed in scarlet red soutanes, capes and mitres, carrying tall pastoral staffs.

Pope Gregory was dressed in elegant white robes and a cape, elaborately embroidered. He walked blindly, flanked by two young assistants. Padre Isidoro, the second-in-command in the Order, leaned heavily on his staff, seemingly burdened with responsibility. Padre Elias, the third-in-command, walked with pride and energy. Having been a flamenco dancer prior to entering the Order he brought all his flamboyance and creativity to his new role: the construction of the cathedral. He orchestrated the extravagant grand events and special feast days.

The procession of floats carried magnificent life-sized statues of Jesus and Mary and other principal figures associated with Holy Week. They were adorned with hundreds of candles and beautiful flowers. Troupes of men, in perfect formation, carried the floats high in the air as they moved to the sound of rousing Spanish marches played by a brass band. The men were hidden behind the skirts of the floats. When the band paused, the soft sound of their shuffling feet was all that was heard in the stillness of the night. They swayed and rocked, tenderly and passionately, in perfect time. The sacred mysteries of Christianity seemed alive and real.

My conscience accused me. I had a past that needed cleansing.

The blood-curdling lament, flamenco-style, of a tenor's solo pierced the cool desert air as he poured out his anguish at the foot of the Cross. Jesus suffered and died to show us the extent of God's infinite love. Was I willing to die a little to prove my love?

In November 1983, thirteen months after I entered the Order, I was given permission to take my first vows – vows of poverty, chastity and obedience – which were binding for three years.

In the intervening months, since the Mother General's reprimand, I had pondered and hurt, and even sulked a bit. Eventually, the Mother General scolded me at the cathedral one night for failing to embrace the true spirit of the Carmelite Order. Also, she said I cared too much about what other people thought.

Whoa! Wasn't I meant to care? However, with that second rebuke, I decided to call a truce and raise my voice, but not my head. My head would stay bowed forever, as a constant reminder of that awful day a few months earlier.

Four other young women who had entered the Order about the same time as me were allowed to take their vows too. During the ceremony we wore identical white dresses and veils, a symbol of purity. We were brides of Christ. Seven other nuns took their final vows that night, with both ceremonies presided over by Padre Isidoro at the cathedral.

In preparation for this event, we attended several classes of instruction with the Mother General – in Spanish, of course. She outlined the basic principles of the vows and the necessity to follow The Rule to perfection. Then she confirmed that we did want to take first vows. She and I were on speaking terms once again. She was doing the talking and I, at least, was able to smile, look her in the eye, and understand a few elementary words and concepts.

After taking our first vows the Mother General gave each of us a crucifix to wear around the neck, a ring to wear on the left hand and a short cream cape to wear during prayers. We were no longer *Hermanas* or Sisters; we were *Madres*, Mothers of souls, the closest experience we would have to motherhood, gained through prayer and penance.

I was keeping my promise, offering my life to God as a gift, as a sacrifice, and fulfilling His command to make reparation. Inside, I was happy and satisfied. I belonged to God and He to me. He knew my past, He saw my efforts, and I trusted Him.

The next day I sat on my bed with a pair of nail scissors and a hand mirror. No one was going to see my head ever again. Short hair was preferable to beat the summer's heat and lack of showers. I took off my veil and head covering, and undid my ponytail.

How short was too short? Better not be excessive. The mirror was too small to be of any use so I started clipping close to the scalp, feeling my way with each tiny cut. As small clumps of soft brown hair fell on the bed, my old life, my old self, slipped further away. I thought of my son and felt sad. Ten minutes later the bell rang for Spiritual Reading and I gathered up my hair, put it in the bin, covered my head, adjusted my veil, and closed the bedroom door. There was no time to sit around brooding – change was afoot.

A new abbey was founded in Seville and nuns from various abbeys, including my own, were moving house. As we stood in the courtyard everyone turned to the Superior.

"Madre Maria Paloma, estás Vice Superiora, aqui," she said.

I could understand those words. She was talking about me. Oh no! She didn't look happy and nor was I. Everyone else looked surprised but not as much as me – I had been named the new Vice Superior in the abbey.

I hadn't been asked if I wanted a promotion and I suspect the Superior hadn't been consulted either. Perhaps the Mother General decided I had learnt my lesson: I had kept my head down, my mouth shut; on the surface, at least, I was chastened, humbled, and submissive.

"Limpiar la casa, Madre Maria Paloma," she added.

"Si, Madre."

In just ten seconds I had gone from the bottom of the Order to close to the top. But I was no longer the cook, I was the cleaner once again – the lowliest job in the abbey.

Later that day the previous Vice Superior moved to another abbey which brought an end to our Spanish lessons – not that the two old nuns and I could speak Spanish – but then we weren't meant to speak anyway.

On that first day, in my new role, I realised I was Vice Superior in name only. The special duties carried out by the previous Vice Superior of washing, starching, and ironing hundreds of purificators (linen cloths used by the priest for wiping the chalice during Mass), went out the door with her. And the Mother Superior decided, despite her heart condition, to climb up and down the stairs to unlock the front door, to ring the bell incessantly throughout the day, and to wake the nuns each morning – rather than delegate any of those duties to me. I did, however, sit next to her at mealtimes, and call the roll, but, in her mind, I was still the last in the Order and not worthy of promotion. I tended to agree. However, I was second-guessing her thoughts – and without any spoken language, I relied on reading body language.

At the next all-night vigil at the cathedral I stood at the top table in the refectory with the Superiors and Vice Superiors. The roll call was read: first the Mother General, then the Superiors in order of promotion, then the first Vice Superior, the second Vice Superior, and then my name. I hardly dared reply. Several nuns coughed nervously because the position of our names on the list had changed, with the order of Vice Superiors now matching that of our Superiors. So, my name disappeared from the bottom of the list and reappeared as number twelve, overnight. I felt like an imposter, especially given my past.

During the washing up, elderly nuns smiled warmly, nodding approval. One squeezed my arm with affection. Several young nuns scowled, as did most of the Vice Superiors. I could understand their resentment. They had been in the Order for years. Some performed their duties and obeyed The Rule to perfection. I had been there only fourteen months. Everyone knew I wasn't a saint. And, as further evidence of my lack of merit, sometimes I fell asleep by mistake. Plus I couldn't speak Spanish. It didn't seem fair.

However, I was in a class of one. At twenty-nine, I was educated and mature while most nuns were too old or too young for promotion. Some had entered as young as fourteen, with little or no education and no life experience, with big dreams of holiness and, probably, big dreams of promotion. The Order was hierarchical and we were constantly reminded of our place, although I had enjoyed being at the bottom of the pyramid. I had a conscience to examine, thoughts to purify, and vows to fulfil.

Poverty was the least exacting of the vows: we had sufficient food, shelter and clothing. Obedience was fulfilled through the observance of the rules and respect for the Superior's authority, both incurring punishment if found wanting. However, the vow of chastity was a struggle but only at night in bed.

Praying with my arms extended, in imitation of Jesus on the cross, was painful but not enough punishment for my body to overcome its sexual feelings. Sometimes I felt disappointed and angry with myself, and with God. He wasn't rescuing me. He wasn't blessing me with buckets full of glorious grace and, thereby, eliminating all my sexual feelings. Oh no! He was letting me experience my fragility and humanity. Late at night, in the quiet, in the dark, sometimes my need for intimacy was unbearable, although I thought that particular craving was only physical and not related to any emotional needs. I was more than a body, and my challenge was to find a way to make it my slave, not the other way around.

I didn't want promotion or the burden of setting a good example as I fended off the evil glare of nuns who pouted and accused. I just wanted time to build my relationship with God. So I kept my head down, eyes lowered, thoughts focused, and hoped it would be sufficient – and that my Superior would warm to me.

Chapter 23
Nightshift

A year later I moved back to the abbey next-door as Vice Superior. I saw this as another promotion and, this time, I was pleased – and relieved that my name dropped three places on the roll. Life was boring, and my relationship with the elderly German Superior had remained stagnant.

The beguiling smile, the inscrutable face, the unbreakable will of the Japanese Superior would be challenging, I knew. Nevertheless, her precise interpretation of the rules would be a welcome change as would her energy and intelligence.

I stepped over the cobblestones and into her abbey. She locked and bolted the door behind me. I fell to my knees. She tossed her veil off her face and blessed me. I rose, she smiled.

"The same cell as before," she said.

"Si, Madre."

I knew where to find it. My second winter in Seville had started with a sharp drop in temperature, overnight, and the shoe-box was going to be freezing but, hopefully, it had two blankets.

The following morning I rang the large bell in the courtyard to wake everyone in the community. Then I walked around the abbey ringing a small hand bell. I knocked gently on each bedroom door and said, *"Ave Maria purissima."* Each nun poked her covered head outside her room and replied, *"Sin pecado concebido."*

I rang the large bell throughout the day.

"You are a minute late," the Superior said on more than one occasion.

I learnt to be very exact with timekeeping because I wanted to please her, not challenge or irritate her as the Indian nun had.

Immediately after breakfast, I cleaned the chapel. Then I washed everyone's personal laundry in the washing machine, before carrying it upstairs and hanging it on the enclosed balcony – the drier being reserved for emergency use only. When the washing was dry, I ironed it before folding it neatly into individual piles. In between those chores, I washed, starched and ironed all the surplices and albs for the priests. I had to remove the red linings before washing and then re-sew them by hand into lace cuffs and waistbands. I enjoyed the work, and I tried to be fast and efficient, winning the Superior's confidence.

On Christmas Eve the baby Jesus was placed in a manger on the main altar and, in true Spanish style, we lined up to kiss His tiny feet in a gesture of love and adoration. After supper that night I wasn't asked to sing solo; nobody sang. Our only treats were tinned ham and confectionery.

Christmas had always been a time of fun, family and festivity with a big singsong around the piano, with boating adventures, sunburn and freckles. Now I was covered in a religious habit from head to toe, looking like a nun, behaving like a nun, and thinking like a nun. I sat at a long trestle table covered in plastic, in a cold refectory filled with a hundred nuns, in perfect silence. The effect of that isolation from family, and absence of normal human interaction, was acute. Talking to God in quiet prayer was my only contact with anyone and, at that time of the year, I longed to speak to someone and express a little happiness.

Back home in the abbey more responsibility awaited me.

" You are going to make hosts, Madre Maria Paloma, with Madre Maria Bianca," the Superior said one morning.

"Si, Madre."

Madre Maria Bianca and I eyed one another. Was she feeling a little apprehensive? She was very young – possibly only sixteen. I was pleased and smiled back.

The tiny old German nun was listening. She nodded, enthusiastically – her sharp eyes willing us to do a good job. She didn't want to be called on to fix things.

It was a privilege to be allowed to make Holy Communion wafers. A few times in the past I had assisted other nuns but never had the full responsibility myself. I hoped the machine was working properly. Burnt and broken wafers were no good for anything.

At 3:45 pm that afternoon, Madre Maria Bianca and I left our abbey. We walked around the corner to another abbey to make thousands of little white wafers. While we worked, we prayed non-stop, reciting the same prayers as at the cathedral. Her voice was louder than mine and I felt humbled that my prayers got softer and softer. My voice was exhausted from leading the singing each night.

Virtue and goodness were equated with physical and vocal strength, and I suspected that many younger nuns thought I wasn't worthy because I wasn't loud enough or strong enough. Night after night, Madre Maria Bianca had the perfect opportunity to compare her efforts with mine.

Host-making was quite a procedure. We made the altar breads from a mixture of flour and water which we beat together with an electric mixer and then ladled onto a hot-plate about thirty centimetres in diameter. The lid of the hot-plate was engraved with religious symbols in the shape of small and large wafers. On closing the lid, the handles on both plates locked tightly together, spreading the ladled mixture evenly over the hot surface. A minute later we unlocked the handles and removed the large cooked wafer. We repeated this process over and over.

The wafers were crisp and tended to curl, so we laid them out individually on shelves in a steam room until soft and moist. Several hours later we stacked them in plastic bags, weighted them down with heavy chopping boards, and left them to flatten overnight.

The following night, while one of us was doing the cooking, the other was cutting each wafer by hand, using a sharp circular cutter which had to be positioned carefully around each symbol. The cutters came in two sizes: large and small.

Cutting wafers by hand, cleanly and accurately, was hard work and we switched roles every hour or two. Later in the night, we examined each wafer to ensure there were no loose particles around the edges. Every single crumb was meticulously removed with lightning speed. Then we counted them before placing them in clear plastic bags. We could cook, steam, prepare and cut three thousand large wafers and five thousand small each night.

We worked for eight hours without so much as a five-minute break, a cup of tea or a sit down. We became immune to pain and fatigue. Occasionally, at the end of the night we compared our hands with a smile but no words. Both our palms were red and badly indented from the force exerted on the circular cutter, but we knew they would recover before the next shift, and only the calluses would remain.

We started clearing up around midnight and, as soon as the nuns arrived from Palmar, we walked home in the dark. The streets were deserted, the cool night air delicious, our arms limp at our sides. But we felt grateful. We were finished for another night. Madre Maria Bianca never complained. I thought her efforts were amazing.

"Ave Maria purissima," we said, as we stepped inside the front door of our abbey.

"Sin pecado concebido," the Superior replied, locking and bolting the door behind us. Then *"¿Cuantos?"* she asked, as she threw her black veil off her face. She didn't look at me. She only wanted to know how many wafers we had made.

"Tres mil grandes, cinco mil pequeñas, Madre Superiora," I whispered.

She nodded her head, avoiding eye contact. She was tired, like we were. Her precise interpretation of the rules obliged her to pray every word and sing every note at the cathedral. She never fell asleep, not even on the return journey in the van. She was the epitome of self-control and discipline. Only her posture reflected the level of her exhaustion – her shoulders were slumped, chest fallen, legs wobbly, and voice destroyed.

Madre Maria Bianca and I were not the only nuns who stayed in Seville to work. Some nuns spent half the night ironing starched altar cloths, and others sewed – all the clothes for the priests and nuns were made by the nuns. Every night suitcases full of dirty laundry came back to the abbeys, full of altar cloths and vestments. The quantity increased when the missionary priests arrived from overseas.

Easter arrived and the cathedral filled with noise, emotion and pageantry. By this stage I knew that twelve months was a very long time in the life of a Carmelite nun. I strained to hold on to the images of Easter especially because I was hurting inside, again.

My parents and sister had come to Palmar de Troya and I was hoping to see them. Unfortunately, I was given permission to speak to them only twice in the ten-minute breaks. I wasted valuable time looking for them outside, among hundreds of pilgrims, because no one had informed them that I had permission to see them. Adding to the difficulty was the fact that my chaperone was riddled with arthritis and unable to hurry. By the time I found my family, the bells were ringing and I had to go inside.

Each night during the grand outdoor procession, my sister walked at my side, crying. Many years later she told me that she felt like I had died.

After Easter Madre Maria Bianca and I resumed the job of host-making. No one ever gave us any feedback on the quantity or quality of our work but, as with everything else in our monastic life, questions and curiosity had to be squashed. To fill the void, I talked to myself.

Months of host-making drained my energy reserves and I looked forward to a night at the cathedral as a chance to rest. Summer was approaching, and groves of ugly olive trees, their branches misshapen and bent, buckled and folded under the intensity of the Sevillian sun. The unchanging image of the olive groves contrasted sharply with the rest of the landscape, which was left fallow most of the year. Recently, however, it had been planted in sunflower seeds.

Young green seedlings were bursting into life, racing skywards; nursing buds, heralding fertility and abundance. Soon the splashes of shimmering gold exploded into a dense, seamless carpet of blazing colour, inspiring inner happiness and vitality.

Contemplating the changing vista of the cycle of life on the ancient floodplains of the Guadalquivir River, I drew comparisons with religious themes: the crucifixion and death of Jesus and his subsequent Resurrection. And our own humble life with unseen, yet glorious, spiritual consequences.

I remembered the parables of the Bible even though I never read the Bible anymore. Nor did I hear it read at Mass in a foreign language because, along with all the other changes Pope Gregory had initiated, he had removed the Epistle and Gospel readings from Mass. Fortunately, the Bible stories were so engrained in my memory that I could easily recall them, especially some favourite ones like the parable of the small grain of mustard seed, the widow's mite, and the pearl of great price. The journey in the van was a favourite time to let my mind wander.

As we drove home at the end of the night, I tried to catch sight of a temperature gauge located on the side of the road in the middle of the city. Usually, in the height of summer, it read thirty-five degrees Celsius.

We wore the same clothing all year round and I was used to my clothing being wringing wet, and my underclothing turning bright orange. Everyone's long baggy pants and singlets turned orange. It was extraordinary to see. A whole year's worth of tomatoes, carrots, capsicums, oranges, red grapes, mangoes and persimmons. So much colour sweated out of every pore.

At the cathedral, we almost ran outside to toss our black veils off our faces and get some fresh air on our skin. Each night in the van we opened the windows as wide as possible to create the maximum draught. The old nuns wanted the windows closed while the young couldn't get enough fresh air. Sometimes a little squabbling ensued as tempers flared amidst the prayers, even though everyone knew that talking was forbidden.

I often wondered what other secret aches and pains some nuns were hiding. My right knee had recently become swollen and infected, and both heels were cracked and bleeding. I had noticed another nun at the cathedral walking on the balls of her feet and I decided she probably had cracked heels like me. The pain was intense, the cure simple, but we were meant to suffer. There was no medicine chest.

At home in the abbey, the Superior and I had settled into an easy rapport. I worked hard and she trusted me. However, once I had mastered the role, my thoughts focused on other things. Many aspects of our life needed adjusting. There was too much emphasis on petty rules but never a mention of charity, kindness or gratitude. Some nuns looked forlorn, others were tired and cranky, but no one, except the elderly and infirm, were ever allowed extra sleep. And, to make life worse, the Superior told us one day at bedtime that we had to take turns to pray the Rosary in the chapel, right through the night.

We stared at one another in horror.

"Why?" someone asked.

"Silencio," she replied. "The Pope says so."

The Germans protested a little more.

"The old nuns can sleep," she conceded. Which meant only the younger generation had to pray.

Shush! Be careful, I thought. *Don't aggravate her anymore.*

I glared at them. *Don't you remember how she punished me a couple of weeks ago, for failing to wake you on time during the all-night vigil? Don't you remember seeing me in the dining room, eating my meals on my knees for a week?*

I remembered. It was humiliating.

"Silencio."

Later that night, when it was time for bed, the first Rosary turn started at 1:30 am and continued for an hour. The other turns followed on, every hour, till 5:30 am. My turn was at 3:30 am.

I went to my room and decided to fill in the time by writing a letter to my parents. We were allowed to send only one letter per month and often it took me some time to think of something to say. All letters in and out were read by the Pope, or his assistant, plus the Mother General and the Superior. I opened my letter-writing folder, flicked through the last letter I'd received from Mother, and then stared at a photo I'd received from the girl who could have been my American sister-in-law: a family photo. Her brother was still single. She believed in signs from God. Had she received a sign? Was she sending me a sign? If so, what? Signs required interpretation so words were easier to understand, but she wrote so little in her letter that I was left guessing.

I put the photo away but decided not to throw it out. He and I had nothing in common but he was part of the reason I was a Carmelite nun; although a small part.

I focused on writing to my parents, my thoughts slow and random. Half an hour passed, then an hour. I told them about the extra Rosary turns. I always pretended everything was wonderful.

At 3:15 am, a nun tip-toed along the passageway, knocked on my door, and whispered my name.

"Si, Madre," I replied.

I returned to my cell at 4:35 am. The alarm rang at 7:00 am and I got up and woke the community. Night after night we took turns to pray till dawn. Each morning I searched everyone's face for signs of desperation or despair. Did I need to worry? To my knowledge, no one had ever died of sleeplessness or fatigue, but they had from a lack of love.

Chapter 24
1 Corinthians

The glare of a street lamp illuminated the driving rain as we stepped out of the van on the corner of *Calle Alfaqueque*. Our socks and sandals, long capes and habits were already sopping wet – a storm had struck earlier in the night. The little old German nun with the ferocious will was the only one with an umbrella. She struggled to prevent it from turning inside out in the wind.

The Superior unlocked the door of our abbey, and we stepped inside.

"There's no electricity," she whispered, flicking the light switch.

As she closed the front door, we were engulfed in darkness.

"Careful," she said, between gritted teeth.

Two nuns from South America muttered to each other. I never could understand a word they said. They seemed the most unlikely women to become nuns. One was old, cranky and almost incapacitated. The other had a terrible temper, and was constantly disobedient and argumentative. I wondered if she was unwell because nothing was ever expected of her.

"Silencio, Madres."

We walked upstairs, feeling our way in the dark, clinging to the handrail with one hand and gathering up our habits with the other. By the time we arrived on the third floor, the Superior had lit a couple of candles. Dinner in the refectory wasn't an option that night – rain was pouring through the ceiling and everything was soaking wet. The rooftop balcony was leaking again.

"Sit on the stairs," the Superior said.

The tiles were icy cold.

We ate dry bread and Granny Smith apples, followed by a glass of cold water. This had been our dinner every night for several weeks – the Pope's latest penance for us.

The candles flickered in the semi-darkness, accentuating the obvious. A young nun from Nigeria shivered uncontrollably. She looked like she was at breaking point: her eyes vacant yet fearful, her expression sullen – such a contrast to the radiant smile and bubbly sweetness which had characterised her first twelve months in the Order. Recently, she had stopped praying aloud.

It had taken some time for me to assess the nuns in our abbey. It was only when I observed change over time, and particularly with newcomers, that I began to get a better understanding of how well we were coping. I was demanding more of myself and I hoped I would be able to keep going and that God would look after me.

Some nuns in the Order seemed to thrive on hyperactivity, throwing themselves into work and prayer, recklessly and boldly. I was in awe of their strength and commitment. A few looked too serious and introverted. Others looked defeated. And, now, at risk – at least, mentally.

I wondered if the Mother General was helping those who were struggling but somehow I doubted it. My observations suggested that Superiors only dealt with enforcing the rules and I tried to relieve the boredom, and sense of powerlessness by thinking of all the wonderful changes I would make if ever I became a Superior.

Prompted by a suggestion from the Mother General, who had told me in confidence of a certain young nun in her abbey who had requested permission to sleep without a mattress, I decided to do the same. I was guessing the hidden meaning behind those words: the choice of a wooden bed over a soft mattress might indeed kill off some sexual feelings. I was ready to give it a try.

The first week was extremely painful and I didn't sleep; instead, I twisted and turned as my bones dug into the chipboard. Lying on my back proved the best option. And it was an excellent exercise in keeping perfectly still while trying to relax.

In time I grew to love the wooden bed. Psychologically, I was reminding myself of my firm desire to be chaste, even in my sleep, which was patchy. This was me, taking control. I was going to conquer my libido, one way or another. *Brazos en cruz* till my arms collapsed, host-making till midnight, asking forgiveness from my Superior on bended knee for insignificant faults, even wrapping my hands in lengths of cloth – everything was a source of motivation to fulfil my vow of chastity. But, still I failed. And, then, I had to humble myself in confession.

Whenever I accused myself, the priest was stern in his condemnation but offered no real advice other than to pray harder and trust God. Sometimes I was questioned as to whether or not I had deliberately sinned, and that didn't help either. How conscious was I in the dead of night? Therefore, how responsible? My Spanish was too limited to delve any deeper.

Nonetheless, I felt let down by God and I was angry with Him. He knew my struggle, my intent, but He never seemed to help me overcome my basic instincts. I had no fantasies about anyone from my past, no dreams about make-believe romance, just a physical urge which I was determined to conquer.

Curiously, Pope Gregory's latest ruling seemed to focus on the same troublesome part of the female anatomy and we were made to wear boned corsets. Since our clothing was loose and flowing, obviously the corset was not meant to make our figures look more sexy, curvaceous or slender. Sometimes I was tormented with erotic thoughts at the cathedral and I wondered what fantasies Pope Gregory had, dreaming about the nuns in corsets. Or was he concerned about protecting our chastity? And, if so, how did that work?

No answers were supplied – but the corset was horrible to wear. In summer it was yet another layer of underwear to create and absorb perspiration. With the corset and suspenders came the requirement to wear thick black stockings instead of socks. I missed the little rush of cool air travelling up my bare legs in the middle of summer when my socks fell down around my ankles.

About this same time, my Superior became sick and spent a week in her room although she never relinquished control of anything in the abbey.

"You're five seconds late with the bell, Madre Maria Paloma," she said in a nasty voice from the balcony above the courtyard.

"Si, Madre." This was the only response I ever made. Anything else would have been deemed punishable.

Her criticism seemed illogical to me, especially considering my workload. Lately, despite my best efforts to please her, she had become even more frigid and judgmental. My only hope of escape from her fixations was a change of abbey.

The Mother General decided who moved where and when, and it seemed to me that these decisions were based on a number of variables: promotion, demotion, work, physical strength, skills, and resolving conflict. Every abbey was a mix of ages and cultures, with sufficient young nuns in each abbey to do the work and care for the elderly.

A few months later I received the news I was desperate to hear: I was moving. At 1:00 pm that day I went to my room, changed into my good habit and packed my suitcase. I was changing places with one of the best nuns in the Order. She was Irish, a favourite with the Mother General, reliable, virtuous and physically strong. But she was exhausted and fell asleep at the cathedral every night.

As I cleaned my tiny cell for the last time, I felt a bit sentimental about leaving it. I had toughened up in this abbey, and proved my worth. I wondered what lay ahead, and if I would be making hosts in the new abbey because the host-making machine had recently been moved there.

At 1:30 pm I went downstairs to the courtyard and rang the bell. Then I tied a thick black veil on top of the maroon veil.

"Are you ready?" the Superior asked.

"Si Madre," I replied.

She gave me directions about how to get to the new abbey. I knelt at her feet and she made the sign of the cross, in the form of a blessing, with her crucifix. Not surprisingly, I felt blessed that I was escaping. I stepped outside, accompanied by two other nuns.

We walked in silence but my thoughts were busy. My new Superior had been a nun for many years in South America before coming to Palmar de Troya. The Mother General had told me that she was kind but tended to favour some and reject others. I hoped she wouldn't reject me.

When we arrived at the new abbey, the small neat figure of the Superior appeared at the front door.

"Gracias, Madres," I said to my companions. "Godspeed."

"Gracias a ti, tambien," they replied.

I stepped inside and the Superior locked and bolted the door, lifted her veil, gave me her blessing and picked up my suitcase.

"No, no, Madre Superiora," I said, trying to take it from her.

"It's okay," she replied, firmly.

I knew that tone of voice.

She shuffled into the courtyard and put the suitcase down beside the sweeping staircase. All the nuns in the community were standing in a semi-circle and drenched in sunlight from the rooftop above. The Superior muttered and pointed to where she wanted me to stand. She walked over to the bell and rang it three times, vigorously.

Being a trained musician my ears were sensitive to sound. As I listened to the tone of the bell I thought it reflected something of her personality. I had lived with nuns whose bell ringing was so loud I cringed every time I heard it. Since the rules forbade any unnecessary talking, all our other senses were highly tuned to pick up information. Hence facial expressions, body language, tone of voice, rustling of habits and even bell ringing could be important indicators. I was alert and paying attention.

There were seventeen nuns standing in the courtyard and, as Vice Superior, I had to say their names for the roll call. Normally I would have kept my eyes down but being new to the abbey and unsure of who was living there, I looked at each nun's face in turn. Some smiled, giving me a nod; others looked away. Were they snubbing me already? One, in particular, snarled, but she always snarled. I had often wondered why; perhaps I would now learn.

After lunch, the day proceeded as usual and we went to Palmar. The following morning my Superior said I could spend the day doing whatever I liked; at least, I think she did. She spoke so quickly I had to guess. Her dark eyes stared at me, unflinching – she wasn't going to explain or repeat herself. This was the first real glimmer I had of her true self, or rather the person she had become given the life we led. I wondered how frustrated she was, hearing her language mutilated by non-Spaniards.

She chatted to the nuns standing in one corner of the courtyard. Everyone ignored the rule of silence as they laughed and joked noisily. No one was in a hurry to start the day's work. I was amazed to see how little they cared about the rule of silence. I could hear my previous Superior in my head, threatening them. I went to the chapel to join the elderly nuns in prayer as it seemed the best way to fill in some time on my first full day in the abbey.

After reciting a Rosary I walked into the kitchen where the Superior was chopping garlic and onions. She was chatting to the cook, passing on the finer points of making *paella* and *patata tortilla*. I had never eaten real *paella* before and I looked forward to tasting it. Thankfully, sardines were off the menu at night, and lunch had been reduced to soup, bread and fruit so mealtimes were less painful.

The Superior wore an apron like the rest of us, with sleeves hooked up, ready for work. I'd never lived with a Superior who helped with the work nor one who wasn't exasperated or limited by speaking a foreign language. I hoped she would continue to surprise in a good way.

She motioned me into the courtyard. She wanted to outline her vision for her community of

Carmelite nuns, she said, and that the only thing that mattered was *la caridad,* love. Of course, I agreed. This was my vision too. 1 Corinthians Chapter 13 verses 4-8 was one of my favourite passages in the Bible; without love, everything else was useless.

I went upstairs to offer my services to the host-making nuns as I tried to remember the Bible verses: *love is patient, love is kind.* I could hear voices coming from the far end of the corridor. *Love isn't envious and it doesn't boast.*

I stepped into the host-making room – six young nuns, six pairs of hands, keen to excel and impress. No doubt, all competing with each other. *Love isn't proud.*

In response to my offer of help, the team leader said, *"Gracias, pero no."* Thanks, but no thanks. Ouch, they didn't need me. Did they know how many hosts I had made? Did they care? What was I going to do with the next two hours? *Love isn't self-seeking.* The host-making team didn't want me and I had to get used to that idea.

As I walked back down the empty corridor I heard their chatter fade – the sound of happy nuns at work. Inside, I felt hollow and emotionally dead. My brain was stuck in a grim dark place, fenced in by rules and controlled by fear of punishment. Yet I was wound up, geared for action, taut and on edge. I needed time to calm down and relax. But how long would that process take? Actually, I was lucky I didn't have to exhaust myself making hosts. Everyone else was smiling and I needed to smile, too. I hadn't smiled in months.

Most mornings I joined the old nuns in the chapel before wandering around the abbey, looking for something to do. On several occasions I asked if I could help with host-making but every time I was turned down.

I felt guilty being so idle. I checked on a South American nun who was blind. She seemed like a saint and I hoped some of her virtue might rub off on me. I wondered how the previous Vice Superior had filled in her days. She was a workaholic, an ironing expert, with a strong arm – a much stronger arm than mine.

About two weeks later, while I was exploring a messy storeroom behind the kitchen, I found a hammer and nails – exactly what I needed to repair the dining chairs. Every chair in the refectory was an accident waiting to happen. The legs and frames were rickety and broken.

I wondered which priest was responsible for buying the second-hand chairs and who had decided not to repair them before the nuns moved in. My brain was clogged with unanswered questions; I was used to being in a state of unknowing.

My Superior gave me permission to start work on the chairs, and the empty storeroom was the perfect workshop. Back home in New Zealand I had helped Dad with boat maintenance above and below the waterline so I knew how to sand, fill and paint. Also, Dad had spent many years in the furniture business, both in retail and manufacture, so I was very opinionated about furniture.

Seeing my progress, my Superior asked what else I needed and a few days later she gave me more sheets of sandpaper, a tube of glue, a box of tacks and a tin of wood stain: in fact, everything I had asked for. I was surprised money had been found for such items. Perhaps the Mother General was feeling generous or wealthy? Usually her response was, *"No hay dinero."* There's no money.

The restoration of the chairs was easy and enjoyable; in truth, I had never felt so happy. I completed the job by reupholstering the seats with scraps of material I found in the storeroom, donated by the sewing department for some other project long before. The elderly German nuns reassured me my efforts were appreciated. They couldn't speak Spanish but their beaming smiles were very telling. Even the Superior seemed pleased. And it helped, most certainly, although I was acutely aware of still being an outsider. My biggest concern was whether or not I was doomed to remain one.

Chapter 25
Gossip and Lies

During Mass each morning the young nuns vied for supremacy as the Trisagio, a prayer to the Blessed Trinity, was recited. Some wanted to lead through sheer speed, others through volume. The noise was ridiculous but the Superior ensured she outdid them.

Each morning after breakfast, conversation continued in the courtyard, led by the Superior. She was determined her relaxed attitude to the rules would prevail and many nuns followed her example.

When the chairs were repaired, I looked around for other things to do. I thought the Superior had accepted me, and valued my contribution, so I was surprised when she reprimanded me one day.

A young nun in the abbey had told the Superior that I had recommended she cure her infected knee by lancing it under the hot tap. I had fixed my own infected knees this way and, it was true, I had suggested she try it.

Unfortunately, the young nun went to the Superior without warning me. The Superior said the nun needed medicine not a pinprick.

"Pardon, Madre," I said. I knew better than to argue the point.

Her words seemed unnecessarily harsh and out of character, making me realise how little I knew about her. The young nun continued to pray on both knees so I deduced they weren't too badly infected. Nevertheless, I was a bit baffled by the Superior's outburst, and, later, disappointed when she told me to move back to the previous abbey as Vice Superior. Of course, no explanation was given.

I was meant to obey, to accept without question. However, I had never managed to suppress the little voice in my head and now it was protesting loudly. As I packed my bag to leave I wondered if, in some way, I had been responsible. The infected knee incident seemed an unlikely cause so I was left guessing.

One night as I walked across the cathedral compound the Mother General motioned to me to approach.

"I thought you should know that I had to move you, Madre Maria Paloma," she said. "The Superior complained that you were disobedient."

Impossible.

"I know from past experience that she uses disobedience as an excuse to get rid of Vice Superiors she doesn't want."

But love rejoices in truth. Love always protects, trusts, hopes and perseveres. How could she justify a lie?

"You weren't disobedient, were you?"

"No, Madre, of course not."

She nodded her head and smiled.

I felt even more disappointed than ever. Our lives were pointless if we didn't try to replicate Jesus' life and principles. Suffering, in itself, wasn't sufficient.

"You were missed in the other abbey," she continued. "Your replacement can't sew."

Small consolation. I didn't even like sewing and I wasn't very good at it. But I was fast, and speed was crucial because there was a lot of work to do.

Deep inside I was longing for a little peace and happiness. I had had a small taste of something different – where love was at least talked about and, therefore, valued. But, once again, I had been sent back to the dungeon, with a prison guard.

The next morning I woke with a headache, which was unusual for me. Other parts of my body often ached from exhaustion but the pain usually disappeared after a short rest or change of activity. So I waited for the headache to go, too, day after day, night after night. Finally, I talked to God about it. And continued to wait.

Eventually, I was forced to tell the Mother General I had a headache after fainting in the cathedral one night. She allowed me to see the doctor who said I had high blood pressure. The female doctor prescribed some medicine for a period of two weeks, but it didn't help.

"It's ya cross, Madre Maria Paloma," the Mother General said. "Ya have to offer it up to God, without complaint. Ya have to trust Him."

That wasn't what I wanted to hear. Our life was hard enough without constant physical pain. I thought I was suffering more than any other person on the planet. And adding to the problem was my inability to sleep at night.

Inexplicably, the Superior never asked me about my health. She had no maternal instincts, and no interest in helping me get well, even though she had been a nurse prior to entering the Order.

The summer's heat turned to autumn bliss but I was stuck in an abbey I had outgrown, with a Superior I found wanting. The pain in my head was so acute I likened it to an angry volcano, ready to erupt.

The conversation in my head went round and round: I had to obey, to empty myself of all desire, to let go, like Jesus did on the Cross. Nonetheless, I didn't want to let go of my own thoughts. They had kept me going for four years – my hopes of changing things for the better. But I needed to get well first.

One night I sat on my bed in my tiny cell, head in hands, feeling desperate and alone.

You cut your hair too short last week.

I know; it's prickly and it hurts.

Final Vows are coming up in a month's time.

I know.

What are you going to do?

Don't know. Head hurts.

You could leave.

My hair is too short.

It'll grow.

What would I do in the world? I've been here so long I wouldn't fit in.

True.

I should stay. Keep my promise to God. Answer His call to make reparation.

And trust Him?

Hmm. Yes, trust Him. I'm getting better at that. But I can't see my way through with this pain in my head.

I know.

I took Final Vows as planned, and waited for God to cure me. I changed confessors again and again. Finally I confided in Padre Frederico, the first time I had ever opened my heart to anyone at Palmar. He told me to have confidence, and to prepare to become the next Superior. I cried, and told him it was impossible; the pressure in the back of my head was killing me.

Over the next few months, tears trickled down my cheeks in confession as Padre Frederico tried to console me. I talked about my Superior for the very first time. He knew all about her, he said. Over the years many nuns had complained about her.

Padre Frederico was so kind and gentle that I even told him the story of my life, about the pregnancy and adoption, and my guilt and shame.

"Don't worry," he said. "God knows."

Another night, in answer to more revelations of mine, he said, "When I was a young seminarian in South America, I seriously thought about leaving but a priest convinced me not to. God knows what we go through and He understands. Sexual feelings disappear as one gets older. Everything will be all right. Prepare to be the next Superior."

Telling me not to worry didn't help me because it didn't fix my headache. I knew I couldn't be a Superior if I was sick. Too many Superiors were grumpy and irritable and I knew I needed to get well before I was given any further responsibility. So I changed confessors again, looking for answers.

A few months later another abbey was founded in Seville. A nun was chosen to be the Superior, and that nun wasn't me. It was no surprise.

I was stuck – not only in physical pain but with an infuriating sense of hopelessness. The only consolation was spiritual: Pope Gregory's sermons and documents were reminding us that the end of the world was near, that suffering was glory, and that martyrdom was possible.

This course of events seemed all the more plausible when we drove into Seville one particular night – the streets were even more deserted than usual. The only traffic consisted of long lines of tanks and armoured vehicles carrying tens of thousands of soldiers on manoeuvres. We stared in horror. Was Spain at war? Was the world at war? Was this the war Pope Gregory had been predicting?

Our prayers got louder as armed soldiers waved us through at each intersection. We were the only non-military vehicles on the road. How was that possible? It was terrifying.

The van stopped at the usual place and we got out and hurried home. During dinner, everyone except the Superior looked scared. I lay awake in bed all night, listening for the sound of bombs or gunfire. Would I die? Would I be a martyr? Death would bring an end to my headache. At 7:00 am my alarm rang.

Everyone prayed louder during Mass that morning, and breakfast was even more serious than normal. After the meal, the Superior said everything was all right and that there was nothing to worry about. I didn't believe her and, I suspect, I wasn't the only nun who didn't.

That afternoon we stared out the windows as we drove to the cathedral. Yet, despite the memory of the terrifying scenes of the previous night, the city of Seville seemed alive and bustling with commerce, just like any other day of the year. Our prayers were recited with as much fervour and intensity as the previous night. Nobody fell asleep on the journey there or back, not even the driver and his companion.

Many years later I learnt that the manoeuvres were part of a combined international military exercise to practise defence readiness. That simple piece of information was so valuable, the difference between understanding and fear, but we, the Carmelites of the Holy Face, were kept ignorant.

Another two years passed.

I was in the sewing abbey as Vice Superior after a tumultuous twelve months, which included six more changes of abbey and several demotions and promotions. I was still nursing a headache, day and night, which sapped my energy and patience but the Mother General didn't want to know about it. Her concern was only for the elderly; plus three or four special cases. I wasn't special so I received no help or consideration.

My new Superior was a Spaniard, with a ferocious will and dark penetrating eyes. I wasn't intimidated – my thoughts were pure, my intentions noble. She demanded strict obedience and humility, and I respected her for that.

I rang the bell during the day and cleaned the abbey – a rambling two-storey house of draughty corridors, sweeping staircases, grotty bathrooms and expansive courtyard.

When I was finished the cleaning each morning, I returned to the courtyard with a bottle of Harpic toilet cleaner and a bowl of water. The white marble tiles in the courtyard were old and grey, and I had decided to clean them properly, one tile at a time. Jif wasn't strong enough but a sprinkle of Harpic, combined with a heavy-duty scourer, was effective in removing years of discolouration. This was superfluous to the cleaning specification but, thankfully, my initiative was tolerated by the Superior.

Every day I got down on my hands and knees, with a long brown apron covering my habit. On some days my arms were exhausted before I started but I kept scrubbing – my happiness dependent on completing one tile per day.

Chapter 26
Alone in my Room

The summer's heat was streaming through the window in my room on the rooftop. A pedal organ stood at the foot of the bed. The room was small, divided in two by a partition and a curtain. Another nun slept in the other half of the space at night.

I was in the Mother General's abbey, demoted again. Someone had complained about me. It would have been so easy to defend myself, to say that the nun was lying, but I didn't. I had been practising silence for too long. I was still striving to imitate Jesus who went to His death without uttering a word.

I stared at the manuscript paper on top of the organ. There was no hurry to compose anything; I had no other day job. For the first time in eight years I was allowed to sit down during the day. I had time to think, undisturbed. It was a unique position to be in.

Every morning, straight after breakfast, I climbed three flights of stairs to the rooftop. No one spoke to me all day. I was completely isolated.

Six months earlier Father Isidoro had instructed the Mother General to form a choir of twelve nuns, and I had been given the responsibility to train them. From 5:00 pm till 5:45 pm each day we gathered in the refectory at the cathedral to practice.

"The next abbey that's founded should be for the choir," a young Spanish nun said as she entered the refectory.

"Shh."

"Madre Maria Paloma! What do you think?" she continued, grinning at me.

It was a great idea. Was it possible that God was listening after all?

Some nuns looked suspicious as they sat down at one of the long trestle tables. Everyone must have been wondering why I had been demoted. Of course, I wasn't allowed to tell them. Others looked deflated and scowled. I tried to be positive.

The same young nun always talked about an abbey for the choir. She wasn't worried about the rules. She was more interested in keeping her dream alive.

Two extra faces joined the choir practice, then another one or two more until we numbered twenty. Our task was to dominate the voices of the other fifty nuns who had been abusing their voices for years, all in the name of obedience.

I had been given two books of old Spanish hymns by Padre Isidoro, and had concluded that the best way to control the singing was to create a new repertoire which only the choir knew. The Mother General had given me some manuscript paper and I had started writing hymn sheets with lyrics and exquisite harmonies. She had them photo-copied, bought plastic folders, and we had the makings of hymn books.

Hidden beneath our black veils it was difficult to read in the cathedral but some nuns were very musical and learnt quickly. I knelt in the back row, tuning fork in hand, with the best and strongest voices beside me.

Night after night I said the same thing at choir practice. "Don't scream. Padre Isidoro wants beautiful singing." In time I was able to add, "I have asked the Mother General for permission to pray without *brazos en cruz* and she has agreed. We need our energy for singing." Everyone nodded. There was a lot of incentive to improve and impress – a new abbey for the choir was definitely a possibility now, and I assumed I was the most likely candidate for the next promotion to Superior.

Back in Seville, a roster had been drawn up for the recitation of non-stop Rosaries during the night, and, once again, our sleep was badly interrupted. I knelt in the chapel at 2:00 am, then 3:00 am and 4:00 am, thinking how absurd it was. The extra Rosaries had been demanded by the Pope, so I had no right to question his judgment; except I did.

About this time, thunderous clouds gathered on the horizon, dumping torrential rain in Seville and flooding the crypt of the public cemetery where deceased members of the Carmelite Order were interred. Recently the crypt in the cathedral at Palmar de Troya had been completed, so the Pope instructed that the waterlogged coffins of the deceased priests and nuns be opened, and the bodies transferred to the cathedral.

When the coffins were opened, some corpses were found to be incorrupt; that is, the bodies had not decomposed despite not being preserved by embalming. We saw this as proof of God's continued blessings on the Order and as proof of the holiness of the individuals concerned.

Alone in my room, my thoughts wandered away from music. My right knee was badly infected again, and I went to the bathroom to put some hot water on it. I pricked it a dozen times with a pin to let the pus out. I made the sign of the cross on it. Then I looked at my heels and made the sign of the cross on them, too. They were cracked and bleeding.

I walked back to my room and sat on the bed. I was meant to be working on music for the choir but I wanted to think. The pain in my head was horrendous but no one cared. Except God.

I sat, brooding. Surely there was a solution to the pain. I turned the spotlight inwards, beneath the layers of clothing, acknowledging the caged mind inhibited by pages of rules and the dire effect of eight years of silence, hardship and sleeplessness.

When I went to the cathedral that afternoon, I allowed my thoughts to wander even more freely than usual. I wondered about the seal of confession and whether or not Padre Frederico had kept my secret.

Another sleepless night followed as we took turns to pray throughout the night. The following day I sat on my bed, again. The room was turning into an oven and there was nothing I could do to keep the heat out. Perspiration was running down my skin, soaking into singlet, pants and corset before leaking into the underdress and the overdress, the head covering and veils. I leant my head against the wall, willing God to have mercy on me, and closed my eyes.

When I went to confession that night I peered through my veil, staring into every corner of the confessional box. Was the Pope listening to my confession? Did he need a microphone or was he able to discern the state of my soul through direct communication with God? I felt bitterly disappointed with myself, and with the life I had led in the Order. Did the Pope know how dejected I felt?

Alone in my room I tried to relive the memory of eight Superiors, twelve changes of abbey and all the associated emotions. My freedom to think had been curbed by rules and rigid timetabling, but I was breaking the rules by not working. My sight had been impeded by a veil but my mind was exploring new ideas. Punishment, injustice and cruelty had wounded my sensitivity and wizened my loving heart. Although I had escaped from that abbey and rejected the negativity of its Superior, I was still battling the effects of that enforced imprisonment.

The moment of truth came with no warning or fanfare as I acknowledged the cause of the pain in my head: my panic at returning to that abbey, four years earlier, where there was no love, no joy, no appreciation. I had felt trapped – my trust in God wasn't that great that I could be His puppet. Life in the abbey did matter to me. The Superior's obsession with the rules and her need to punish were destructive – and I objected.

Time slowed down as my mood changed. Pencil and rubber remained untouched on the organ beside the manuscript paper. I sat on the bed and closed my eyes to block out the stark white walls of my cell. To block out the intense heat streaming through the window. I closed my eyes so I could see beneath my skin and find myself – my other self, an old self, a different self.

I cared too deeply – about this life, these rules, these people. Yet these people didn't care about me.

The bell rang downstairs. I would have to save further analysis for another day. I would stay with that last thought: I cared too deeply. But it wasn't right *not* to care. Surely?

Another journey to Palmar de Troya, another sleepless night. I cared too deeply. The same internal conversation, day after day, night after night.

The nun who slept on the other side of the curtain never stirred throughout the night while I lay wide awake. The only sounds came from the street below or the rooftop next door: foreign sounds, unintelligible. Hardly a distraction from the pain in my head. From the torment, like torture. Or from the curiosity of what lay beneath my skin.

Slowly, invisibly, the caring eased. The nerves calmed as my thought processes unravelled, and then spiralled into fantasy: my body was filled with insects. Yes, that made perfect sense.

A new focus: how was I going to rid myself of insects? Did the insects represent the pain in my head? My need to find a cure. To eradicate, eliminate.

Indifference replaced my concern. And the pain vanished. But would the pain return? Could pain be related to thought? To feeling? More panic, and the pain returned; the connection between both so fragile, yet so critical to my wellbeing.

I cared too deeply.

Stop caring!

Pencil and rubber continued to lie side by side on top of the organ, untouched.

Stop caring!

Another week. Another all-night vigil. Utter exhaustion, mental and physical.

I wanted to find peace, to hold onto peace, and never let it go. I was looking through a portal, a tunnel that was leading to a new consciousness, a different understanding of myself and my life in the Order. But where would it lead? The veil and cloister had been my refuge, home, family and world – an escape from my past, an entry into God's kingdom.

Jumbled thoughts searched for insight and direction. I knew that some Palmarian believers thought Pope Gregory and his top aides, Padre Isidoro and Padre Elias, had the special grace of reading people's minds. That idea seemed plausible, and I even convinced myself there were microphones tuned in to every word we said in confession.

Humiliation, correction, punishment and scorn had silenced my voice, crushed my spirit and left me broken. Yet, paradoxically, in the isolation of my rooftop bedroom, as I became more irrational, I found some hope.

Obsessed by a need for change and a desire to be heard, I wrote a letter to Padre Isidoro outlining my concerns about our life. I was going to the top, by-passing the Mother General: she was ineffective. I folded the letter and placed it on top of the organ, feeling satisfied. Doing so was purely a gesture as I now believed he could read it without entering my room.

My mood was brighter that day, the journey to Palmar faster, the ceremonies shorter. After the final roll call of the night, I climbed the stairs to my room, eager to see what had happened to the letter. However, it lay on top of the organ exactly where I had left it, unopened, untouched. I was puzzled.

As the noises in the abbey became softer and less frequent, each nun turned off her light and fell asleep. I turned off my light too, and lay in the dark, thinking as always. My letter hadn't produced the response I was expecting but I was, finally, pain-free. Gloriously, fabulously pain-free. That was something to be happy about.

The next morning I was forced to admit my theories must be wrong. I had been expecting some sort of sign that the letter had been read, but there was no sign. My logic was faulty. It had to be.

Over the next few days I had a heightened sense of futility as I considered the foolishness of my life in the Order. All the doubts I had fiercely tried to squash were fighting to be heard anew, and now I was providing no answers nor justifying anything. The blinds of my consciousness were beginning to open.

Chapter 27
The Vision

The Mother General and I were sitting outside the cathedral, side by side, our black veils billowing in the breeze. We could hear the nuns' voices floating through the arched doorway. I'd never heard the choir from a distance before. It sounded beautiful.

"I don't believe in Palmar anymore so I want to leave the Order," I said.

I waited for her to reply, but she remained silent.

I was trying to make sense of Palmar de Troya and its self-appointed Pope. I had believed the story for ten years, without any concrete evidence – faith is blind and religions are based on faith. My life had been built on faith and, now, I was tearing it apart. My reason for coming to Palmar was driven by my need to punish myself. That need had been fulfilled.

I told her about my life: the pregnancy and adoption. Brief and sanitised. Her bottom lip trembled in horror as she gasped.

"I'm convinced my body is riddled with insects," I confided.

"But why?"

"Because it is."

I thought my honesty would illicit some response but she had nothing further to say, no insight to share, no words of comfort or wisdom – only a command that had to be obeyed. "You must not enter the cathedral, Madre Maria Paloma. Wait outside until the ceremonies are finished. Do you understand?"

"*Si, Madre,*" I replied.

She stood up, lowered her black veil over her face, and walked away. I gazed at the night sky, peppered with stars. My watch ticked slowly, second by second. A black cat sauntered past. It sent shivers up and down my spine. Had I seen that cat before? Maybe, maybe not. I didn't know and I didn't care.

I glanced at the gated wall of the compound. A baby appeared, dressed only in a nappy. He crawled in and out through a hole in the concrete block wall. His pale skin and soft blond curls shone in the moonlight. Why was a baby there, all alone? It didn't make sense. I thought of my own son.

I looked at the wall again and the baby had disappeared. I remembered the primary reason for coming to Palmar de Troya and the voice I had heard in my bedroom at home: God's voice. I had fulfilled God's requirement to 'make reparation'. I had punished my body, crucified my mind, purified my heart and soul. I had paid the price for my sins, for abandoning my baby.

I would miss the austerity of the cathedral's cold stone, the remoteness of the desert landscape, the cloister of the black veil, the detachment from everything, the annihilation of self, the oneness with God.

There were some extraordinary women in the Order and I knew I would miss them, too. We had been companions on a spiritual journey, united in a religious belief, willing to dedicate our lives, to shed our blood, to be martyred for the cause if necessary. Yet everything had changed for me, alone in my upstairs bedroom, and I had to leave. I knew I would never see them again.

I returned to Seville that night as usual. The Mother General said someone would bring my dinner upstairs. She forbade me from talking to anyone, or leaving my room, except to use the bathroom. I was an outcast.

Two days later she told me to accompany her to the Pope's residence where I was to have an interview with Padre Isidoro. When we arrived there we knocked and slipped our veils over our faces. The door opened and we stepped inside. The Mother General spoke to the priest on door-duty, then waited in the entrance while he escorted me across the courtyard to Padre Isidoro's office. He knocked, and I stepped into the room.

Padre Isidoro was sitting behind a large wooden desk cluttered with books and papers. I noticed the books in particular because I had missed having real books to read. The nuns only had the Book of Rules and Pope Gregory's documents, all of which were serious and frightening. It didn't seem fair that Padre Isidoro had other books.

He told me to sit down. He was a handsome man, with a Roman nose and small dark eyes. He was dressed in a black soutane with a scarlet watered-silk sash and skull cap. There were thirty-three scarlet buttons running down the front of his soutane, representing the thirty-three years of Jesus' life – very symbolic, I thought. I wondered what significance Jesus had for him? His allegiance was to Pope Gregory XVII.

He asked me why I wanted to leave.

I peered into his face from behind my black veil, feeling overwhelmed by a sense of evil. This man had supported Clemente Dominquez Gomez, Pope Gregory XVII, from the very beginning of the alleged apparitions at Palmar de Troya. He had previously been a lawyer. He was the Pope's eyes and ears. The administrator. He was crucial to the success of the Palmarian Church.

Either he was part of the deliberate deception of thousands of Catholics or he was tricked by his friend, Clemente. If he had been tricked... why was that? Was he stupid? A fanatic? A religious zealot? Or filled with grandiose ideas about his own importance?

I felt disheartened and lifeless. I listened to my voice, hoarse and broken, to words that had a will of their own, that said unimaginable things about not believing in the Palmarian Church any longer.

He offered no words of advice, comfort or gratitude – just like the Mother General. What was the matter with these people? Had they forgotten how to be human? It seemed absurd.

Who was this man? Why had I trusted this Church so implicitly?

He gave me permission to leave the Order and I thanked him and left.

On returning to the abbey, air tickets were purchased, and two days later I was allowed to leave. I took off my habit, piece by piece, kissing each article of clothing. I kissed my crucifix and ring, symbols of my vows, one last time. And then I removed my corset for the very last time.

I dressed in a tailored blue suit, a white blouse and headscarf that had been given to me by the Mother General's assistant. Fortunately, my hair wasn't too short.

I put on a pair of sheer stockings and pinned them to my long baggy pants with the only safety pins I had: two pins on the left leg and one pin on the right, which was obviously going to fall down all the way home. But I didn't care. There was no way I was going to wear a boned corset and suspenders ever again.

I left the abbey without saying a word to anyone. I had no luggage, only a shoulder bag containing my Bible, writing pad and passport.

The Mother General and her assistant accompanied me to the airport in a taxi, in silence. At the airport I thanked her.

"I will never forget what you have taught me," I said.

She handed me the air tickets and a little money. "Padre Isidoro says you're not allowed to phone your family until you're out of Spain."

"Si Madre," I replied.

The plane landed in Madrid and I spent the night at the airport, counting the hours till dawn. Someone had organised an itinerary without any thought for me. Of course, the Order wasn't concerned about sleep deprivation. They just wanted to get rid of me as soon as possible.

My immediate focus was my parents. I knew I would have to be very convincing to get them out of the Palmarian religion. In my absence they had gone so far as to buy a church, south of Auckland, and even had a resident priest.

What would it take to persuade them to give it up?

Chapter 28
Letting Go

As I walked across the tarmac my stockings started falling down but there was nowhere for me to hide. I sighed, feeling embarrassed.

Keep your head up, pretend everything is fine and, maybe, the air hostess won't notice.

She smiled sweetly and checked my ticket. Phew! The plane was almost empty, the journey from Madrid to Japan quiet and peaceful, the upholstered seat comfortable and soothing. I gazed out the window at the vast blue pristine void, willing the surreal beauty of aeronautical travel to envelope me and take me away. I wanted to let go, to surrender to its power.

When we arrived in Japan I located a public phone booth and rang my parents. Mother sounded pleased to hear I was coming home, although I pretended I was still a nun. I didn't want her to worry, and I didn't want to be accused of causing an asthma attack or an argument.

In reality, I didn't have a clue what my status was; whether my vows were binding or not and, therefore, if I *was* a nun in any sense of the word. One thing was certain: because I had left the Order after taking final vows, I was excommunicated from the Palmarian Church.

My parents promised to meet me at Auckland Airport the following day, and I ended the conversation without further delay. With that job done, I headed to the bathroom – it was time to remove the scarf from my head. I stood in front of the mirror and looked at myself for the first time in eight years. Staring back at me was an image I didn't recognise, of an older woman who appeared serious and pale. I gazed into her eyes, noticing some wrinkles and that her hair had lost its golden brown tinge. I'd never seen myself with short hair before. I smiled at her and she smiled back. We knew one another quite well.

I splashed handfuls of cold water on my face, and patted it dry with soft paper towels. Then I fiddled with the scarf. It was navy blue cotton with a silver thread. I decided to get rid of the veil look. There was no need to cover my head any longer. I tied it around my neck; it felt nice and soft.

Later that day another plane took me home to Auckland. Although I don't remember precisely what day it was, it must have been the beginning of August 1990. I didn't even know the date at the time. I was thirty-seven years old but thirty-seven meant nothing. I felt more like a hundred: old, tired and worn-out.

Yes, I was repeating what I had done once before. I was coming home to my parents after another failed convent experience. And I was poor. Just like the first time. But this time I felt I had completed my task: my soul was cleansed, my debt paid, my conscience clear.

As I walked through the exit I saw not only my parents, but most of my siblings, their partners and young children, plus a new sister-in-law.

"Maria," they cried. I'd forgotten what it felt like to belong to a family.

Mother and Dad hugged me first. "Hello, darling," they said. "Welcome home."

Was I home?

"Hi," I said, moving from one to the other for more hugs and kisses. I couldn't think of anything else to say. My brain felt like a machine that hadn't been turned on in years, my lips the cogs that were jammed.

"It's good to see you."

I repeated their words. I listened to myself, to the unfamiliar accent, not like the old me, pre-Palmar de Troya.

"What about your luggage?" someone asked.

No tengo, no tengo, I thought. "I don't have any."

I sounded like a robot. Everyone looked surprised.

We walked through the airport and out to the car park. The sun was shining, the temperature a cool 12 degrees C, a pleasant change from the 50 degrees I had left behind in Seville.

The family had decided we would go to Damian's house – he lived closest to the airport – so a convoy of vehicles headed out of the car park, bumper to bumper. My distant memories reminded me that convoys were for funeral processions. That was a sombre thought, but at least it was a thought, and it was my thought.

I sat in the back seat of my parents' car.

"You're still a nun, darling?" Mother asked.

"Yes, Mother. I'm home for a holiday." The robot voice had resurfaced as I translated in my head, word for word.

At some point I had to tell them the truth, but not yet. Had I lost my religious vocation? Had I turned my back on God – again? I wasn't a Carmelite nun and I didn't have a religion. So who was I? I had no idea. Deep inside I felt a huge nothingness.

At Damian's the kettle was boiled, plates of cakes appeared and everyone started chatting excitedly.

"Maria, so much has happened in the world while you were away in Spain," Damian said. "I've made a list of ten important events to tell you about."

I looked at my brother blankly. Why would I care about world events? I had been saving the world for the past eight years by prayer and penance. I hadn't seen a newspaper or a television in all that time. But I had seen the city of Seville geared for war, deserted but for thousands of troops, tanks and armoured vehicles that were on manoeuvres through the city centre. That image was still firmly fixed in my brain.

"I really can't decide what is the most significant event on a global scale but I'll start with the collapse of the Berlin Wall last year." Turning to Dad he asked, "You heard about that, didn't you?"

Dad nodded in agreement as he licked his fingers covered in sticky crumbs of sponge, jam and cream. I remembered that Dad had always enjoyed fresh cakes.

Damian then proceeded to share his list, which included the nuclear plant disaster at Chernobyl, the sinking of the *Rainbow Warrior* and the Tiananmen Square protest.

"And number ten is the fact that there is a deadly virus called Aids which is killing people. Scientists don't know where it came from or what causes it, but they suspect it started with monkeys in Africa."

It was meaningless to me. Mother offered me another piece of chocolate cake and I was surprised it was tasteless, just like the first piece. I hadn't eaten cake in years and it should have been delicious but it wasn't.

"And here's something that might interest you in particular, Maria. American nuns who are old and retired are offering themselves as guinea pigs as part of a research project to find a cure for Aids. They're being injected with the virus, offering their lives to medical research. Very noble! That's something you could consider," he concluded knowingly.

'Offer myself as a guinea pig.' I heard the words repeating in my head. I wasn't much use for anything else. I was empty. I was nothing. I wondered what it would feel like to die a slow painful death in a drug trial. Of course, I had been dying – dying to myself – for eight years. Death by Aids would be another step in the same direction so it was a possibility, something to consider.

"Tell us about Spain, Maria, about the life you lead over there," someone said.

Everyone was looking at me but my lips didn't know how to move. I paused and stumbled. I tried to tell them about staying up all night – praying.

About the exhaustion, the hunger pains, the stiff legs, the infected knees, the sore throats, the 'no medicine' policy. Short blunt sentences. Basic words. Translating in my head as fast as I could. But my fast seemed so slow. I was counting the seconds. Each second was interminable. It was agony.

"You should get some counselling after all you've been through," Damian said.

You don't have a clue what I've been through. I'm strong. I survived.

I stayed in Auckland for a few days with my sister, Erica, and her family. She bought me some underwear and gave me clothes from her wardrobe. I had a shower, and washed off three days' dirt and eight years of washing out of a bucket of lukewarm water.

Erica fussed over me and cooked me tasty meals while I stood in the kitchen feeling awkward. I didn't know what to do with my hands and arms. For years they had been busy working and extended in *brazos en cruz,* or tucked neatly under my cream scapular. Now they had nowhere to hide, nothing to do. As Erica filled in the silences with her chatter, I counted the hours till bedtime.

When I lay down to sleep that first night on a mattress, I thought I would miss my wooden bed, but I didn't. I thought I would sleep for hours and hours, making up for all the sleep I had missed, but I didn't. Instead, I hardly slept at all. I thought about the nuns in Seville. They were the only people with whom I felt any emotional ties. Even though we had hardly spoken, we had been bound together by a religious belief and the sharing of an extraordinary life – the life of a Carmelite nun in a breakaway religious sect.

The following morning I ate toast, butter and jam instead of dry bread and cheese. I remembered only too well how much I had missed butter those first few days in the Order, but I had quickly adjusted.

"Dry bread is delicious," I said.

"Really?" Erica replied.

I felt emotionally detached. Everything had changed so quickly, like the flick of an on-off switch. The memories were alive and real, from just a week before or a month before; yet they seemed to belong to another time, another person, and I was cut off from them. From the moment I had taken off the Carmelite habit, I had severed my connections with the Order and I wasn't a Carmelite nun any longer.

At the end of the week, my parents arrived and took me home to the Waikato, eighty kilometres south of Auckland. On the journey home I told them I had left the Carmelite Order. They let me talk without interrupting. Much of what I said was illogical – the ramblings of an exhausted woman, suffering from anxiety and sleeplessness.

Chapter 29
Conflict at Home

The church property my parents owned bordered a farming community. They had worked hard renovating it, and had created accommodation for themselves in part of the church hall. Everything was freshly painted, the grounds recently mown and flower beds in bloom despite the winter's chill.

They said they prayed every day and every night, even staying awake for an all-night vigil each Saturday, aligning themselves with the nuns and priests at Palmar de Troya. Their commitment to the Church was as great as mine had been.

Mother boiled the kettle as we sat down around the dining room table. Afternoon tea turned into dinner and then supper. There was eight years of catching up to do.

Initially, I did a lot of the talking. I was determined to convince them that the Palmarian Church was not the Church they thought it was, simply by sharing my personal experiences with them. Dad questioned why I had stayed so long, given the lack of charity and cruel punishments. These were indicators that the Holy Spirit was not guiding them as they proclaimed, he said. I was surprised he was willing to see the other side.

Dad's own concerns were with the rules that Pope Gregory had enforced for laypeople, rules so strict that believers were discouraged from socialising with non-believers, even within their own families. The rules required that anyone who visited them had to dress according to Palmarian rules.

Apparently, my siblings and spouses objected to the dress code and consequently rarely visited. This was news to me. Dad said he felt alienated from his own children, while Mother had tried to convert them, relentlessly bombarding their letterboxes with religious newspapers.

"The more she persists," he said "the more they resist." He looked sad as he rested his elbows on the table, running his fingers through his comb-over.

Despite their efforts, Dad and Mother had managed to convert only simple-minded, uneducated migrants in New Zealand. Their best results had been during a trip to Samoa and the Philippines to establish the Palmarian Church there.

However, Dad's biggest query was with Pope Gregory who, despite portraying himself in his documents as a holy man of prayer, had presented quite differently when he arrived in New Zealand with his entourage of Cardinals.

"The Cardinals were drunk," he said.

"What?" I could hardly believe it.

"And they turned down the accommodation I prepared for them in our hall – at considerable personal expense, I might add."

"Really?"

"They said they only ever stayed in five star hotels when travelling overseas."

"Wow!" What an admission. "We lived in utter poverty."

Dad looked disgusted. It was obvious my parents lived a very frugal life with no luxury of any kind. Perhaps I would be able to get them out of the Church without too much difficulty, although Mother seemed less critical than Dad. Absolute certainty in a belief system that guaranteed eternal salvation, for her children and all poor sinners, had given her great peace of mind. I could appreciate that. Even her asthma seemed better.

I was worried, though. They were visibly older despite their energy and stamina. Dad was seventy-six, Mother seventy-two.

Dad said he had sold his investment properties and given everything to Pope Gregory.

"But why?"

Before I left for Spain I had spent dozens of hours looking at real-estate with them, and making sure their investments were sound. I had even helped them renovate a basement double garage and turn it into a cosy chapel. It seemed that as soon as I had left, Mother had set about changing everything. In fact, my parents had bought two church properties, one in Auckland, the other in the Waikato. However, they had sold the one in Auckland because the congregation was too small.

"Mother insisted we give everything to the Pope," Dad continued.

"So you've got nothing aside for your old age?"
"Correct."

I stared at Mother. She looked very happy with herself. I knew my siblings would be furious and probably blame me.

"And we've given the title of this church to Pope Gregory," he concluded.

It seemed impossible to understand.

"We trust God," Mother said. "He'll look after us."

In my experience, that was a gamble.

"It's harder for a rich man to get into heaven than for a camel to get through the eye of a needle," she continued.

"You know that's not the meaning of those words," I replied.

"Whatever little money we have left from our government pension each month, we use to buy second-hand tools and clothing to send to the Palmarian believers in the Philippines. They're very poor over there, and they really appreciate anything we can send them," he said.

"That's very generous of you," I replied, lowering my voice a notch. I knew I needed to keep on side with them. "But things are different now, Dad. I don't believe in the Palmarian Church."

Dad and I exchanged glances. The moment of truth had arrived.

"I can't disprove the original heavenly messages at Palmar de Troya, or the so-called miracles, or Pope Gregory's stigmata, but I have lived in the Order. I know the way things are done over there and it doesn't make sense to me anymore."

Mother was standing at the kitchen bench, biting her bottom lip – something she often did.

I needed to push on while I had their attention.

"None of Pope Gregory's predictions have been fulfilled," I said. "The world has not been converted."

They couldn't deny that.

"I've never felt better," Mother said. "I'm focused on heaven and on saving souls for God. That's all that matters to me."

She was the same little woman: resolute, big-hearted, committed. I had to admire her courage and selflessness.

"That's wonderful, Mother, but I still think we've been deceived."

We sat quietly for a while. I knew that even if I managed to convince them of the false claims of the Palmarian Church, they might have to walk away from it with nothing but their clothing and a few pieces of furniture.

It had been a very long day but, now, it was time to go to bed. There would be many more discussions before we reached any agreement, if that were even possible. Dad said he would ring his lawyer in the morning to see what they could do to have the church property returned to them. I made a mental note to remind him. My brain was starting to wake up.

Life with my parents proved challenging. I felt an urgency to communicate as much as possible to them about my time as a Carmelite nun. This forced me to speak English. We spent entire days and nights around the dining room table, talking, while Mother continued to resist. She loved her life of prayer and self-denial. Once she even threatened to leave Dad if necessary, her commitment to God was so great. Dad was distraught. However, I became more determined. Palmar de Troya had taught me to be strong.

My only priority was to convince Mother that Pope Gregory was a fraud. Her marriage to Dad depended on it. I wasn't going to see him alone and unloved in his old age, especially after everything he had sacrificed for her and her religious beliefs.

Finding evidence from within the Palmarian Church, from Pope Gregory's own papal documents, seemed the best approach, and I devised a plan that I hoped would work. I needed to present any plausible evidence of fraud to an independent authority. I suggested Father Denzel Meuli, a traditional Roman Catholic priest, who held two doctorates. She knew him from her childhood, and she respected him.

Fortunately, she took the bait and accepted my proposal, and I started reading for ten hours a day, which focused my thoughts on something concrete and forced me to be objective and clinical – things which had been absent from my life for many years. As part of my research I read every document I could find on the Palmarian Church, making notes on anything that looked suspicious or false.

Two months later I presented my findings to Father Meuli. He agreed that some of Pope Gregory's statements were in direct conflict with traditional Catholic teaching. In particular, he stated emphatically that Pope Gregory could not rescind or annul the power of any priest who didn't acknowledge him as the true Pope. He stressed that God would never jeopardise the salvation of his people by inspiring a Pope to carry out such a threat, simply because a priest refused to accept him as the legitimate successor to St Peter. He said no Pope has that power. So Pope Gregory couldn't possibly be the true Pope.

He questioned the reasoning that prompted Pope Gregory to make such a wild pronouncement. Was it fury, meanness, spite or delusion? Mother listened quietly, allowing herself to be convinced by his argument. Dad and I nodded, feeling relieved.

I asked about my status as a nun and he assured me that Pope Gregory had no authority, except in his own opinion, to accept and bind anyone to religious vows. So I wasn't a nun and never had been. Surprisingly, I didn't have any reaction to that. Still, I didn't react to much. My only goal was to get my parents out of the Palmarian Church. I didn't have any sense of self. Who was Maria? I didn't know.

As we drove back home I wondered why we hadn't consulted Father Meuli ten years earlier, before we abandoned the Roman Catholic Church. At the time, many of the changes promulgated by Vatican Council II appeared to be in contradiction to tradition so it had been easy to abandon the Church. But our situation had been different then. I had returned home from Melbourne poor, needy and pregnant; the consequences of that first convent experience still raw for my parents and me – consequences that would be eternally irreparable.

Back home in The Waikato my life was quiet and peaceful – the perfect tonic. A few weeks later I visited the local Catholic Church and spoke to the parish priest, telling him my story from beginning to end. He listened kindly, inviting me to come to Mass and join in parish life. I asked if I could play the church piano when no one else was around and he said I could.

As the fog and frost of the Waikato winter eased to warm spring days, my thoughts wandered away from the rigid rules of the fanatical religious leader in Spain and his Carmelite Order. I knew I had to take some determined steps to assimilate back into society but, as yet, I had no desire to do so.

I started running each day along rough country roads, mile after mile, paddock after paddock. It was good to feel the breeze flying through my hair. I was focused on getting fit and healthy. A few weeks later I started work in a local orchard, picking berries.

Looking to the future, I dared to hope, sensing the need to fight the urge to do nothing. My instincts had been manipulated to keep me cloistered for eight years. Those instincts had to change.

Chapter 30
Back to School

In the New Year I bought a car on hire purchase and moved up to Auckland to start teaching in a Catholic high school. It seemed like the obvious choice – a safe choice. I stayed with an old friend of my parents.

I was awkward at school. I had no small talk. I didn't want anyone to know anything about me, except the principal in whom I had confided a few scant details about having been a Carmelite nun in Spain.

I had tried to eradicate eight years of living behind a veil – faceless, mute, expressionless – in just six months. It was a huge task. But once I had started that process, it had to continue, for my sake and the sake of my future, if I was to have one.

After the silence and discipline of the Carmelite life, the classroom was rowdy, the girls unruly, and me, Miss Hall, terribly serious; a trait I overcame with help from my students.

Sometimes unintelligible words jumped from my mouth as my brain struggled to speak English. The students stared at me. I stared back. Oops! So they were listening after all.

"I'm just like you," I said. "English is my second language. I used to live in Spain and I've forgotten English. That word I just said was half Spanish, half English."

Their faces brightened up. Miss Hall wasn't crazy after all.

"Tell us some Spanish, Miss."

"I'm sure you already know some Spanish words, like *maňana, gracias, adios.*"

"That sounds cool."

The naughtiest and prettiest girl in the room was suddenly interested.

"Yeah, Miss, can you teach us some more?"

"Spanish is way better than French and Maori, Miss."

"Why can't we learn Spanish?"

Wow! They wanted to learn something from me. That was a breakthrough. Usually they sat in class ignoring me. And I couldn't blame them. I knew I was boring but, now, I had found a way to identify with them, and they had seen the evidence first hand.

The following day everyone in the school seemed to know that I could speak Spanish. They rushed down to the music department, a dilapidated old house on the edge of the playing field, squealing and laughing with excitement.

Unprepared as I was for working in the real world with no veil to hide behind and no book of rules for reference, my new principal became my biggest critic when she told me to resign halfway through the first term.

"You don't fit in, Maria. I want you to resign," she said.

I stared at her in dismay. Obviously, she had no idea how hard I was trying. I was straining to become a human being, to have some reason for getting out of bed in the morning. Professionally speaking, I didn't think I had done anything wrong. So could she pressure me to resign?

She had summoned me to her office, unexpectedly. She had a witness at her side, another teacher. His face was expressionless. What had she told him about me? What did he think of her tactics? It was two against one.

I glared at her in defiance. I desperately needed the job. There was nothing else in my life.

"You don't fit in, Maria. I want you to resign," she repeated.

"I'll leave when I'm ready," I said. It was all I could think to blurt out.

I looked down at my clothes. Nothing fitted properly. Everything I had was hand-me-downs, mostly from my aunts. Would I ever fit in – anywhere?

Ordering me to resign only reinforced in my mind that I was an outcast. But it also forced me to stand up for myself. I wasn't a Carmelite nun anymore, and I wasn't about to behave like one. I had to open my mouth and defend myself, difficult as it was.

As I left her office I thought about my first day on the staff at her school, the 'teacher only' day, held at a Catholic retreat centre nearby. A senior male teacher had propositioned me that day. He'd suggested a naughty weekend away, somewhere private. Did I have a cabin we could go to?

"Do you want some?" I had asked as I offered him the milk and sugar. Obviously he'd thought I was offering him something else. But why? My past was still so present that I imagined there was a sign over my head screaming 'ex-nun', but he must have thought I looked all right. In some ways that was reassuring although I spent the rest of the year avoiding him. Four years later, when I did resign, I was ready to move on.

In the meantime Pope Gregory had relinquished the title of the church to my parents, and they sold the property, bought a house in Auckland, and I moved in with them. They chose not to return to the Roman Catholic Church but joined a Latin Mass group instead. An elderly priest administered the group. He was a traditionalist, clinging to the vows he had taken on his ordination day which gave him authority to celebrate the Latin Mass for the rest of his life. Supported by a small number of disaffected Catholics, he lived with his followers and celebrated Mass in their homes. This sort of arrangement was happening all over the world.

I lived with Dad and Mother for two years until Mother told me to leave. She needed to be obeyed and I argued too much. It took a push from her to make me leave because I had always loved home and family life. However, I needed to find an identity of my own and to experience some sort of self-determination, which wasn't possible while I lived under her roof.

I moved into a lovely apartment in a grand old house, with pressed steel ceilings, chandeliers and silk drapes. Within a few short weeks I stopped going to Mass on Sundays, although my head was still full of Catholic doctrine. I continued to pray each night as I fell asleep. It was comforting to think that God did exist, and that He cared. I continued to talk to St Anthony each time I needed a parking spot, and to say the prayer of St Francis of Assisi – *Lord, make me an instrument of your peace* – a prayer I had recited all my life.

My feeble attempts at socialising had improved. A Friday night prayer group had been replaced by an attic bar, a solo guitarist and a glass of red wine. My sister, Erica, was determined to help me move on but, mostly, I sat and stared. I felt more like a shy teenager than the hundred-year-old woman who had stepped off the plane in New Zealand only a few years before.

Despite having punished my body excessively in Spain, aggressively squashing my libido, my emotions were reawakened and sexual feelings returned. Erica introduced me to a man she knew and, after a slow start, we got together. He seemed appropriate in many ways: single, highly educated and with a Catholic background. I dismissed the negative things about him believing my love would overcome everything. However, it couldn't overcome his lack of affection for me. I was a convenient friend – non-judgmental, non-demanding, and easy to have around. After the third break-up, I refused to be available anymore. Despite all my training to be a submissive woman, something inside was finally shouting, "Enough!"

The summer of 1994-1995 was long and hot. Even though I was single, and unemployed after resigning from teaching, I felt optimistic about the future. Physically, emotionally and psychologically, I was better adjusted than ever before.

When a close family member asked me to go into the commercial cleaning business with him, I said I would. Being in business, and self-employed, sounded good – no classroom walls, no domineering boss.

Six months later when his health collapsed, causing him to abandon the business partnership, I found myself in business on my own – the last thing I wanted. Two weeks earlier he had agreed to a contract for a builders' clean of eighty-eight new apartments in the city. If I were to save the business, I would have to honour that contract and all the other contracts we had, which included cleaning offices, cafés and bars.

I put on a brave face when I met the site boss the next day. Dressed in shorts, tee-shirt and running shoes, my normal cleaning clothes, I looked lean and fit. I knew I needed to be convincing, not like an ex-teacher but, more importantly, not like an ex-nun, although I was confident the ex-nun label had fallen off. I had been back in New Zealand five and a half years.

The interview went well and I informed the construction boss that I would return the following day to start work. I drove home and fell into bed. I'd been cleaning throughout the previous night, and I needed to sleep.

Around midnight, I headed out to work again. I drove into the city to do my regular jobs before arriving at the construction site at 9:30 am, ready to start work there. The business was in its infancy but, with no business partner to share the load, I now had far too much to do.

At lunchtime I walked up the road to the university office of Student Job Search. A few minutes later I exited with two young Chinese men. They were perfect, and wildly overqualified for cleaning. One was a pathologist, the other an engineer, but their qualifications were not recognised in New Zealand and they were retraining. They introduced me to their friends and soon I had a small team who were willing to work for ten dollars an hour before tax.

Often I cleaned eighteen to twenty hours a day, seven days a week, occasionally spending forty-eight hours in one long stretch. It reminded me of my life in Spain, although that life was even more punishing. That life had taught me not to put boundaries on anything. I needed to get back into that mind-set. Life on the construction site was tough and rough. We, the lowly cleaners, were at the bottom of the heap.

As a result of that construction contract, I made friends with a wonderful Iraqi family who were refugees. Most of them spoke little or no English, but their pride in their heritage and determination to succeed in their new country provided me with many keen workers over many years. This enabled me to walk onto the biggest construction sites in Auckland city and quote for the builders' clean.

In between construction jobs, my schedule slowed down and I used the time to catch up on lost sleep. As the business became more financially sound I stopped cleaning and became a full-time supervisor of a team of fifteen to twenty employees. I put staff into all the regular office cleaning contracts I had cleaned alone five times a week, and I terminated the awful café contracts. I was tired of chasing café owners who wouldn't pay their cleaning bill.

As cleaners, we came and went in the middle of the night: unseen, unheard, unappreciated. Our hours of work were unsociable, the job strenuous and dirty. Risks of accidents and security breaches were high but the wages were low. Honesty, diligence and reliability were essential qualities and difficult to find, although completely undervalued by most clients.

I relied heavily on my staff to do their job and they relied on me for letters of introduction, support with immigration issues, loans, and financial assistance. I was present for their weddings, births and funerals. One baby was even named after me because the husband absconded and the wife turned to me for financial support. My staff didn't know that my bank account was mostly overdrawn because many clients didn't pay me on time, but I paid my staff each week and supported them as much as I could.

Each one of my staff had an extraordinary story of survival, hardship and endurance that crossed international boundaries, religion, politics and cultures. One was present at the Tiananmen Square massacre, another involved in the Tamil Tigers' fight for freedom, and several at the toppling of the Saddam Hussein regime. They had left family and loved ones, looking for opportunity, peace and security. Compared to their lives, mine was easy.

Books on business covered my office desk. Subscriptions to journals and courses started appearing on bank statements. I joined a mentoring programme for small business owners, which provided me with expert advice. Finally I had the professional support I needed with office systems, business plans and client contacts.

My life was relatively uncomplicated and, more importantly, it was mine. I was still single because I was being cautious. I didn't want another failed relationship.

With no partner to consider and no pressure from religious beliefs, I was free to think in new ways. In time, I even allowed myself to think about my adopted son.

Chapter 31
Becoming Human

Sunday afternoons invariably entailed a visit to my parents. They had moved to a small townhouse, not far from the beach. As we sat around the table, Dad and I talked business while Mother refreshed the teapot and buttered more scones. Afterwards we went for a walk along the beach.

The rest of the family hardly ever saw them so I tried to fill them in on the 'who' and the 'what'. My siblings needed them to apologise for years of harassment but Mother wouldn't. She thought she was a better person for the Palmar experience and Dad wasn't very good at finding the right words. So, the rift caused by the Palmarian Church was never forgiven or forgotten – plus the family fortune had been given away, never to be retrieved, and that was hard for my siblings to accept.

"You must do something about your son," Mother said one day, without any warning.

"It's not up for discussion," I replied.

"It's not right," she insisted. "You're his mother."

"It's my business, not yours. Leave it alone."

I still wasn't ready to face my past head-on, although I was getting closer. As the business expanded, my confidence grew, and I was assuming a new identity.

Ninety per cent of New Zealand businesses employ less than twenty people, and most of those businesses start at home, in the garage. Fifty percent of new businesses fold in the first year, with another fifty per cent in the second year. I had survived those first two critical years. I was a small business owner, the backbone of the economy, providing people with real skills which they could use for the rest of their lives. Some of my staff were so empowered they were going into business on their own which, in turn, helped me feel useful and successful.

So, with that shift in thinking, I was ready to face my past, and dial the number for Child, Youth and Family, a department of New Zealand Social Services.

"Hi, my name is Maria," I said. "My son was adopted in Australia about twenty years ago. It was an open adoption but, until now, I haven't tried to get in contact with him. Can I do that now, after all these years?"

"Yes, you can," a woman replied. "However, because he's over eighteen, legally he's entitled to decline your request to meet him. Did you know that?"

That was a terrible thought – that he might refuse to meet me.

"No, I didn't," I said.

Although I had abandoned him at birth, I was hoping he would want to meet me. I hoped he would understand, somehow, just how difficult it had been for me.

I fiddled with the telephone cord, wondering what to say next.

"Girls are generally keen to meet their birth mothers and, sometimes, quite early in their teens," she continued. "They want to know what she looks like, what her hair is like, what perfume she wears. Boys, on the other hand, often wait till they're in their thirties, when they're happily married with children or planning a family."

This was news to me.

"Boys are more matter-of-fact. They're interested in their medical history, if there are any diseases in the family they need to know about."

I thought about Mother's asthma and Dad's skin cancer issues.

"Would you like me to send you some information on adoption and the path to 'reunion'? There's quite a lot to think about before you take the next step."

'Reunion' seemed like such a peculiar word to use. And 'birth mother' sounded horrible.

"Thanks, that would be great."

We talked for a few more minutes and she said I could ring her at any time. I thanked her, hung up the phone, and swivelled around in the chair, feeling excited that I had finally taken the first step.

I wandered into the kitchen to boil the kettle, knowing that I would have to tell my siblings that I had a son. But not yet; not until I was certain I could meet him. I couldn't bear the pain of telling them only to find out later that he had refused to meet me. I couldn't bear to think of their pity. I didn't want pity.

A few days later a package arrived from Child, Youth and Family. It contained a list of recommended reading and a series of articles covering all aspects of adoption: the sense of loss and rejection, the guilt and shame, the grief, the crisis of identity, the issues around intimacy and control. For the first time I learnt the phrase 'adoption triangle' referring to the birth parents, the baby and the adoptive parents. The more I read, the more complex it seemed, but the more determined I was to understand all facets of the adoption triangle.

Finally, I decided to write a letter to the adoption agency in Australia and request permission to contact my son. A couple of weeks elapsed before they informed me that they had sent him a letter, telling him that I had made contact with them. They said they would let me know, one way or another, when they heard from him.

Every day I drove down the road to the post office box to check the mail, and every day I kept positive, quietly hoping, telling nobody. This was my secret, for me alone. In the meantime, I kept myself busy with work. It was a long twelve months of waiting before he contacted the adoption agency and said I could write to him; any correspondence, however, still had to be via them.

I spent two weeks composing a letter to him. I wanted to give him a sense of who I was but without alarming him. I told him nothing about being a nun or an ex-nun or a Carmelite nun. Instead I wrote about growing up in a big Irish Catholic family in New Zealand; about boats, music, teaching, and owning a cleaning business. I sent him some photos of myself and then I waited for a response, month after month.

Eventually his adoptive mother sent me a card, saying all was well with Zac, as she called him, my son. She said he had started writing a letter to me on the computer but it wasn't finished. Of course, I was thrilled.

I told my siblings the news, but they had news for me. My secret wasn't a secret after all. It seemed that Mother had kept my letters from Melbourne and they had been found and read, the news of my pregnancy secretly shared, years before.

Initially, I felt upset that Mother had ignored me and not destroyed my letters. However, deep inside I knew her love for me had outweighed everything else. She would have read them over and over. It would have been her life-line to me during those long months of waiting for the birth. At least, now, there was no secret to protect any longer.

How sad it was to think that I had been ashamed of being a mother. What had prompted those feelings? Religious rules created by celibate priests?

It was time for me to be more daring and I confided in some friends, none of whom were Catholics. Of course, they were surprised but delighted and, most definitely, not accusing. They had stories of their own – of failed relationships, unplanned pregnancies, lost children, adopted in-laws. They understood. Suddenly I felt human, a feeling I had tried so hard to squash, to eradicate, to deny as a budding nun and a Carmelite nun. It was wonderful to finally join the human race.

When Zac's letter arrived six months later, I realised he was not much more than a boy. I had forgotten what it meant to be so young and naïve.

When we spoke on the phone a few weeks later it was the happiest moment of my life. It was as if my joy was in direct proportion to the level of pain, guilt and shame I had felt for so many years.

Six months later I stood at Auckland airport with my sister and her partner, ready to meet him. I searched every face, shape and posture, looking for something familiar, but he wasn't there. The crowd coming through the exit thinned and stopped, and we continued to wait.

"Is he here?" Erica asked, looking around at the straggly crowd. She was feeling anxious.

"No, not yet."

"You'll have to ask someone," she said. "Maybe he missed the flight."

"Of course he didn't. He would have phoned."

Minutes later a young man emerged on his own. He was handsome, with long dark hair and a good pair of shoulders.

Perhaps that's him, I thought. I only had photos of him as a young boy so I was guessing what he might look like as a young man.

"I'm going to ask him," I said to Erica, nodding in his direction..

"Don't be stupid," she replied. "That's not him."

I ignored her and walked over to him. "Are you Zac?"

"No," he said.

"Sorry."

We waited a few more minutes. Then Erica tugged my sleeve. "Over there," she said. "That's him."

"How do you know?"

"He looks like you."

And yes, he did.

Over the next two weeks he met the family – my nephews felt such a bond they thought they had found a long-lost brother – and he and I toured the country together. It was as if we had never been apart.

It was difficult to know what to tell him because I didn't know him well enough to gauge his reaction to the truth, and I didn't want to confuse or hurt him. So I fabricated a story of studying music in Melbourne in 1977, and of meeting his birth father, who I said was a nice man. I wanted him to feel positive about his biological parents. Then I told him I had been a nun for eight years in a breakaway Carmelite Order in Spain, paying the price for my sins, although I revealed little else of my history.

I had dealt with the pregnancy, birth and adoption, knowing the facts and the people involved, whereas Zac was handed that life as an adopted baby without any choice. He had grown up without any answers; probably fantasizing, like many adoptees do, about his birth parents, and about being rescued, loved and secretly wanted.

Unlike the woman who miscarries or whose baby dies at birth, the woman who gives up her child in a secret adoption often cannot talk about that child to anyone. Her conversations are internalised, although for me, at least, any thought of my baby had been supressed – until now.

For the mother who gives away her baby in a secret adoption, there is no birthday celebration, no reminiscing, no grave to visit, not even any sharing of her sadness. She has given her baby away and she is meant to get over it, just like that. Her baby loss is hers and hers alone. For many it is a silent sorrow.

It is a similar story for the adopted baby and the adoptive family. Everyone is meant to get on with life and be happy. Adoptive mothers aren't meant to grieve their lost chances of carrying their own children full-term. And nor are their husbands.

And what about the lucky baby? He is meant to be grateful for his wonderful chance of being with a family who want him, who choose him. He's not meant to misbehave, voicing his unhappiness or confusion.

I was beginning to appreciate something of what I had done in giving up my child for adoption.

Over the next few years Zac visited New Zealand several times, both on business and on holiday, occasionally staying with me in the house I had bought on Auckland's North Shore. Long hours of cleaning and supervision had earned me the right to take out a mortgage on a little piece of paradise. Finally I had a place of my own – not quite the houseboat I had dreamed of owning as a teenager, but it was a house on the water's edge, surrounded by native bush and wildlife and awash with brilliant sunsets by night.

I lived there on my own, although I had a partner, Cameron, who came and went to suit himself. He was a complex individual with a sense of fun. I employed him to do the accounting for the business although, at one point, he arranged for a colleague, called Nicholas, to set up a new computer system in the downstairs office. Little did I know how important that connection would be a few years later.

I worked long hours, seven days a week. Some of my clients worked fifty-two weeks of the year so my staff and I worked all year round, too.

During the summer of 2002-2003, my parents moved in with me after Dad was diagnosed with stomach cancer. His dying wish was fulfilled when the family reunited around his bedside. He died, aged eighty-nine, a soldier to the end – selfless, generous, and courageous.

A few months later Mother fell and broke her hip and, while in hospital, her welfare was assessed and questions asked about home life. Since the rift in the family between Mother and my siblings had never been healed, no one was willing to help me with her care. Her medical condition was complicated by asthma, heart issues, osteoarthritis, dementia and, now, a hip replacement and walking frame.

Since Dad's death she had enjoyed the novelty of driving around the city with me as I visited the staff each night, but her inability to walk made that impossible, while the dementia meant she could not be left alone at home. It was a difficult time because I had promised myself that I would attend to my parents' needs, except I knew I couldn't do that anymore. For the next eighteen months, until her death, Mother lived in a Catholic rest home, in the bedroom beside the chapel.

Dad's death and Mother's convalescing put some distance between us in a new and positive way. In time I was able to appreciate the real impact of their influence and my inability to be honest with them about religion, out of fear of hurting them.

I asked little of friends and family, being accustomed to listening to others and fulfilling their needs rather than attending to my own. I convinced myself that I was happy even after the first overseas holiday of my life ended in disaster – Cameron didn't travel well with a companion, even one who paid her own way. He ended the relationship in a fit of anger, without any warning or provocation, and I returned to New Zealand with laryngitis. Although he apologised and I forgave him, a month later, he ended it again, in anger. Normally, I was the one cooling his temper after an encounter with someone else. Now, it was my turn to be on the receiving end of his runaway ego, and I resolved never to let it happen again. Being dumped twice in one month, in two different countries by the same man was a record – even by my unconventional standards.

A few weeks later he arrived at my door, boasting he had found the perfect partner.

"What makes her so perfect?" I asked.

"She can't speak English," he replied.

I had been replaced by a woman who couldn't understand a word he said! What did that say about me? I needed answers, and I decided to find a counsellor to help me. As I flicked through the telephone directory the following words jumped off the page: *So you think you're savvy but sometimes don't know what to do.* That summed me up perfectly and I picked up the phone and rang Clare Murphy.

The counselling was brief but intense as I poured out my story, trembling with emotion. I heard the phrase "power and control" for the first time in my life. After each session I drove to the beach and sat in my car, a white MX5, too distraught to move as I pondered the implication of that phrase for me.

Three weeks later, Clare flew to Australia to do her doctorate and I was left to brood. I spent hours in my kayak – the rhythm of long deep strokes through choppy waters, buffeted by strong sea breezes, strengthened my resolve. As the kayak slipped under the Greenhithe bridge, past Herald Island, heading north, my thoughts unwound and recrystallized.

By avoiding conflict and confrontation I had, unknowingly, set myself up for abuse. By being constantly pleasant and accommodating, even when under attack, I had made myself defenceless and vulnerable. For thirty years I had convinced myself that my noble aspirations were worth the sacrifice, but now, at fifty-one, I was alone.

I took the crucifix Mother had given me for my fortieth birthday off the bookshelf and laid it down flat on its back. The symbol of Jesus nailed to the cross was one symbol I had to put aside. The innocent lamb led to the slaughter, as a sacrifice to God, would not be my inspiration anymore. It was keeping me silenced.

I was desperate to express something else. I wanted to value other thoughts. But how? And with what consequences?

Chapter 32
Togetherness

I was hungry for new friends. It was Christmas, time to celebrate, and I used the opportunity to meet clients and acquaintances. The conversation quickly turned to holidays and relationships, and I started to talk about my own failures.

"But you're a successful business woman," one client said. "You're assertive with your staff. I've heard you."

"I used to be a Carmelite nun, remember? I just told you that story."

"But you're not anymore. If you can do it in business, you can do it in your personal life. It's really no different."

Her confidence in me was reassuring.

Wherever I went I continued to talk about what had been, and what could be, hoping that my words would find a new power and become my reality. For the first time in thirty years I became proactive in building healthy relationships, taking full responsibility for the outcome, rather than relying on a God to make things happen for me. The arguments about whoever, whatever or however God did, or did not exist, were no longer relevant. If there was a God somewhere, I was content to leave Him alone.

I encouraged other people to share their ideas with me and, in the process, my life changed. Nicholas offered to do the accounting each month, in place of Cameron, and we soon discovered we had a lot in common. He was at the crossroads, like me, and we supported each other. As our friendship strengthened, we decided to move forward together. From our first night, I slept soundly and peacefully, something I hadn't managed to do since first going to Palmar de Troya – twenty-three years before.

At the end of that year Nicholas bought a yacht: a lifetime's dream for him, from his earliest childhood memories in England, finally realised. For me, it was an opportunity to pick up where I had left off as a twenty year old, when I sold my boat before joining the community of nuns at Loreto Hall.

During our first summer together we explored many beautiful anchorages in Auckland's Hauraki Gulf. Waking up in a bay of our own, on Sunday morning, was more therapeutic than any church service had ever been.

In the New Year, we visited Melbourne. We walked the streets of Camberwell, through the market, past the library and the church of Our Lady of Victories. Standing on the footpath outside Kadesh, my body ached as I relived those distant memories.

We crossed Burke Road, hand in hand, and wandered along the street where Carlos had first spied me. It was harrowing to be there but it was time to dig up the past, and start the grieving process. The only emotions I had consistently acknowledged were guilt and shame and that is where I had remained firmly stuck. Throughout the years I had suppressed everything else. On rare occasions that suppression had welled up in unexpected outbursts of intense anger – inappropriately and without real cause.

However, I was in a new relationship with a different kind of man; one who didn't try to silence me or change me but, instead, encouraged me to explore my past. He wasn't ashamed of me. He wasn't scared of me, or my strange responses which could see me turn into a lifeless statue and become mute as I disappeared behind an invisible Carmelite veil – seemingly frozen in fear or confusion.

In 2007 Nicholas suggested we go to Spain – he thought it would be good for me – and, in time, I agreed. First we went to Valencia to see New Zealand's top yachtsmen compete in the Louis Vuitton Cup and the America's Cup. Then we visited England, his homeland, and Northern Ireland, my ancestral home, before arriving in Seville.

Everything in the 'old quarter' of Seville where I had lived seventeen years before was exactly as I remembered it. Narrow cobblestone streets, terraced housing, iron bars and shutters. However, everything looked a little fresher, recently repaired, newly painted. The drab, muted colours were not quite so bland.

After an hour of nostalgic wandering we came across two dusty streets I knew: *Calle Alfaqueque* and *Calle Abad Gordillo.* We stood outside the very doorways where I had lived as a Carmelite nun. It was amazing to be there.

An hour later we found number four *Calle Almirante Ulloa*, the last abbey I had lived in. The front door was open and a ceramic plaque at the entrance was inscribed with the words: *Residencia Universitaria Santa Ana.* The building was empty and being refurbished. The nuns didn't live there anymore. We stepped over the threshold to the sound of men working at the back of the house.

The spacious courtyard was drenched in sunlight. My mind exploded in images of nuns standing in silence, waiting for the bell, eyes lowered, hands hidden. I remembered the courage and commitment, the undeniable goodness – and the disdain and struggle.

Nicholas and I climbed the marble staircase to the rooftop where my room had once been – each step a step back to times long past. The renovations and fresh paint had done nothing to obscure the memories. Nevertheless, I was terrified someone might appear and question me. Someone might recognise me. I had no right to be there. I was trespassing. I had to get out of there, fast.

A few days later we hired a car and drove to the cathedral of Palmar de Troya. In my absence, motorways had been extended and tiny wayside shops expanded. Once or twice we had to backtrack, as road works blocked our access and I mistranslated road signs.

We stopped for a glass of wine in the village of Palmar de Troya: red wine, to calm my nerves. I needed a drink. Previously I would have associated red wine with Holy Communion, with

Jesus' blood spilt on Calvary, with spiritual sustenance. Chilled white wine would have been more appropriate that day. It was 40 degrees Celsius in the shade.

La taverna was crowded. The locals glared; obviously, we were tourists. The village of Palmar de Troya was popular for only one reason: the imposing cathedral dwarfing their village. We gulped our wine and left. The once humble village was now a thriving town of noisy activity, blaring radios and speeding motorbikes. A few hundred metres further up the hill we parked the car again.

I had tried to prepare Nicholas for the 'Palmar experience'. I knew that once inside the cathedral he was on his own, segregated on the left-hand side with the men, while I would be on the right with the women.

The wall around the compound looked hideous. The iron gates clanged open and we stepped inside. Even though I was scared of being recognised and ordered to leave, I felt ecstatic to be there with a friend.

Once inside the cathedral he was waved through by the Cardinal on the left. The nun on the right told me to zip up the collar of my black jacket. I tried to look through her veil as I listened carefully to her voice. She was reprimanding me in Spanish.

She pointed to the back pew and told me to kneel down. I was petrified. My heart was beating so fast I thought it would smash my chest open. Could she hear it? Would she recognise me – Madre Maria Paloma, an imposter, disguised in a long black dress, black jacket, floppy hat and sunglasses?

She wouldn't let me walk into the cathedral proper because I wasn't wearing the official Holy Face scapular. Obviously, she decided I was a tourist not a believer, and because she was in a position of authority, she was going to stop me from entering her church. I felt sick. I hated her petty rules, her fanaticism, her excessive need to control.

Above the drone of vocal prayer coming from the nuns' stalls at the front of the cathedral, I listened to her prayers, and I recognised her voice. She was Madre Maria Candelaria. Her observance of the rules had always seemed faultless. She was Spanish. We had shared the room on the rooftop at number four *Calle Almirante Ulloa*, the room divided by a flimsy partition and curtain, the room from which I had exited the Order.

I knew I must not speak. If I could recognise her voice, then she most certainly could recognise mine. Then she would order me out of the cathedral before I had had time to look around. I had spent years of my precious life praying in that cathedral. I was part of those brick walls and tall columns, those religious ceremonies and lofty aspirations, and I just wanted to recapture the feeling for a moment or two.

A few minutes later the communion bell rang, and she stood up and walked down the aisle as a procession of nuns appeared at the front of the cathedral. Their black veils billowed around them but I couldn't identify their individual shapes. I stood up and walked outside, overcome by panic and the need to escape. I reminded myself that I no longer believed in Palmar de Troya as a holy place of apparition so there was no need to be sentimental – nor did I accept the simple answers that religion provided to life's big questions.

Standing outside, the walls of the compound seemed oppressive, reminding me of the life I had led, blind and mute.

Nicholas, where are you?

I was pacing up and down.

Seventeen years had elapsed since I had left the Order. I recalled my last night at the cathedral, and the image of a baby crawling through a hole in the wall. It was a beautiful image, one I will never forget; an unexpected hallucination, reminding me of what I had lost.

Nicholas appeared a few minutes later and we walked down the slope together.

"Let's get out of here," he said. "This place gives me the creeps."

"Me, too," I replied.

On the journey back to Seville we talked about the voice I had heard all those years before, in my bedroom, the voice which gave me the impetus to go to Spain. For many years, I had blamed God for tricking me into it, and I had felt angry and confused. Now, I accepted that there had been no voice and that my imagination had given me a message I was desperate to hear. I had been focused on God to show me a way forward, to the exclusion of everything else. I should have been focused on healing Maria, and giving her absolution, not persecuting her.

In time, Nicholas and I planned to make another pivotal trip, this time to visit Zac, my son, in Australia. It was time to tell him the truth. I no longer wanted to hide. Instead, I wanted to treasure my past.

Acknowledgements

Numerous people have generously supported me in the writing of this book. Dr Clare Murphy and Sarah Pickens provided some positive comment in the earliest stages of writing. Paula, Judith, Ann, Sally, Tim and Caroline read with interest. Tina Shaw and Thomas Lodge, provided valuable assessments, Cate Hogan content development, and Stephanie Dagg editorial suggestions. Nicholas Abbott, my partner, listened with patience and encouraged me to write. I am grateful to them all.

Glossary

Act of Contrition: A Catholic prayer that expresses one's sorrow for one's sin.

Alb: A long white garment that covers the priest from head to toe.

Altar rails: A set of wooden railings that separate the altar area – the sanctuary – from the rest of the chapel. At the time for Holy Communion the communicant kneels at the rails.

Angelus: A Christian devotion or prayer which honours Mary and the conception and birth of Jesus.

Apparition: A supernatural event/appearance of a heavenly creature.

Bayside: Veronica Lueken, a Catholic housewife, of Bayside New York purportedly received messages from Our Lady and other well-known saints from 1970 until her death in 1995.

Benediction: Or 'blessing'. It occurs when the priest blesses the congregation with The Eucharist – the consecrated Host – at the end of a period of adoration.

Brazos en cruz: Spanish for 'arms on cross'.

Bi-location: The ability for a person to appear in more than one place at a time.

Capuchin monk: A monk of the Capuchin Order, an off-shoot of the Franciscan Order of Saint Francis of Assisi.

Carmelite: A member of the religious order of Our Lady of Mount Carmel dating back to the twelfth century, on Mount Carmel in Israel. Their primary focus is contemplation.

Christendom: The Christian world.

Clerical collar: A detachable collar that buttons onto a clergy shirt. It closes at the back, creating a seamless front, and is usually white, against a black shirt.

College of Cardinals: The body of all cardinals of the Church.

Confession: A spiritual practice, and a means to holiness, whereby a person confesses his sins to a priest and asks for forgiveness.

Confessional box: A small room or cubicle where confession is held.

Consecration: The moment in the Mass when the bread and wine become the body, blood, soul and divinity of Christ.

Epistle: Extract or short reading taken from the letters of various Apostles to the early Christians and contained in the New Testament of the Bible.

Excommunication: Censure from participation in the full life of the Church due to sin or unacceptable behaviour contrary to Church law. The offender is barred from receiving Holy Communion.

Exposition of the Blessed Sacrament: A simple ceremony in which the Blessed Sacrament (the Eucharist or consecrated Host) is displayed in a monstrance – an ornate gold/silver display case – and placed on the altar for adoration. It usually occurs in the context of Benediction.

Formation: The process by which a new candidate is introduced to a Religious Order and learns about the spiritual, apostolic, doctrinal and practical elements associated with that calling.

Franciscan robes: The traditional long tunic of the Franciscan Order is usually brown, black or grey, and with or without a hood. Small differences exist between the various Orders dedicated to Saint Francis.

Garabandal: Our Lady and Saint Michael the Archangel are said to have appeared to four young schoolgirls in Garabandal, Northern Spain from 1961–1965.

Glory be: A short prayer of praise to God.

Good Samaritan: A parable told by Jesus in St Luke's Gospel in which a traveller, who may or may not be a Jew, is robbed, beaten and left to die. A priest and then a Levite pass by but ignore him. Finally, a Samaritan comes to his rescue. Jews and Samaritans generally despised each other and this parable illustrates the extent of the love that God asks of us.

Gospel: The Bible contains four Gospels attributed to four apostles of Jesus; namely Mathew, Mark, Luke and John. The Gospels detail the life, death and resurrection of Jesus.

Grace: A free gift from God which allows the recipient to share in divine life. Grace can also be received through the sacraments.

Grace at mealtime: A short prayer said before and after a meal, asking for God's blessing on those present and on the food.

Guadalupe: In 1531 a man, called Juan Diego, is said to have met the Virgin Mary on a hill in Tepeyac, near Mexico City. The Virgin performed various miracles, including a painting of herself on the peasant's cloak. The cloak is displayed in the Basilica of Our Lady of Guadalupe in Mexico and is the most visited Marian shrine in the world.

Habit: A distinctive set of garments traditionally worn by members of Religious Orders. It usually consists of a tunic in a drab colour, with a scapular, and a hood for men, a veil for women.

Hail Mary: A traditional Christian prayer asking for Our Lady's intercession. It forms the basis of the Angelus and the Rosary.

Heresy: Offensive belief or theory that is in violation of established religious law.

Holy Communion: Also called The Eucharist and The Lord's Supper – a concept based on Jesus' words to his apostles at The Last Supper. On the night before He died on the Cross, He broke the bread, representing His body, and gave it to His apostles; and shared the wine, representing His blood.

Holy Communion wafer: A thin round unleavened wafer made from fresh white flour and water.

Holy Face scapular: A Roman Catholic devotional scapular based on the Holy Face of Jesus and associated with Veronica, the woman who wiped Jesus' face as He carried the cross to Mt Calvary. Tradition says that Jesus blessed her by imprinting the cloth with His face. Pope Gregory XVII enlarged the scapular and bestowed numerous blessings and graces on the wearer.

Holy water font: A small vessel, often shell-like and with religious decoration, that sits, stands or hangs at the entrance of a church. Visitors bless themselves with the water – making the sign of the cross on forehead, chest and shoulders – on entering and leaving. The water has been blessed by a priest. Some pious Catholics hang a font in the home and bless themselves on entering and leaving.

Holy Week: The week immediately before Easter.

Host: A small round wafer that has been consecrated or blessed by a priest during Mass, thus becoming the Body of Christ.

Infallible: The Pope is infallible when he is exercising his office as teacher and shepherd of the flock while defining doctrine on matters of faith and morals. Papal infallibility was defined as doctrine by Pope Pius IX (1846–1878).

La Salette: The place where Our Lady appeared to two French children in 1846. The apparition was approved by Rome.

Latin Mass: The liturgy of the Roman Catholic Church celebrated in Latin. It usually refers to the Tridentine Mass, dating back to 1570 and Pope Pius V.

Lent: A solemn period of six weeks prior to Easter. A time of spiritual preparation which can include fasting, prayer, self-denial and almsgiving.

Levitation: The raising of the human body into the air by mystical means.

Lord make me an instrument of your peace: A prayer falsely attributed to St Francis of Assisi.

Lourdes: A small town in France where Our Lady appeared to Bernadette Soubirous in 1858. Every year millions of people visit Lourdes and many miracles, officially recognised by

Rome, are said to have occurred there through the consumption of or bathing in the healing waters of the grotto.

Magisterium of the Church: The authority which lays down the true beliefs or teachings of the Church. That authority is vested in the Pope and the Bishops.

Mass: The central act of worship of the Catholic Church in which the Sacrifice of Calvary, Jesus' death on the Cross, is offered to God in an unbloody manner.

Mitre: A tall folding cap, worn by a bishop, and consisting of two identical parts (the front and back) rising to a point and sewn together on the sides. Two short lappets, like wide bands or ribbons, hang down the back.

Monastic life: It developed in early Christian times and involved living alone, in seclusion, away from the world, and practising asceticism. Gradually monasteries were established where people could live an ascetic life in a community.

Mortal sin: A serious sin which if not confessed will result in the soul going to Hell for all eternity. It is so grave that the soul dies and the link with God is severed.

Novice: A prospective member of a Religious Order who is being tested for suitability of admission usually after an initial period of postulancy.

Novice Mistress: The nun who is responsible for the training of the novices and the development of their character in prayer, meditation, Scripture, Church history, the vows and the constitution of the institute.

Opus Dei: An organisation that was founded in Spain in 1928 by a Catholic priest named Josemaria Escriva. It teaches that everyone is called to holiness.

Our Lady of Fatima: A title for Our Lady based on Her apparitions to three young children in Portugal in 1917. Fatima has received official approval from the Catholic Church.

Our Lady of Mount Carmel: A title for Our Lady in Her role as Patroness of the Carmelite Order. The first Carmelites were Christian hermits living on Mt Carmel in the Holy Land during the twelfth century

Our Lady of the Pillar: A title for Our Lady based on Her appearance, through bi-location, to the apostle James circa 40 AD. Mary appeared to James at Zaragoza, standing on top of a pillar, promising him that he would convert his pagan listeners and that their faith would be as strong as the pillar on which she was standing. She is the Patron Saint of Spain.

Padre Pio of Pietrelcina: (1887–1968) An Italian Capuchin priest who bore the stigmata during his life. He was canonized by Pope John Paul II in 2002.

Palm Sunday: The Sunday before Easter which commemorates the entry of Jesus into Jerusalem on a donkey.

Papacy: The office of the Pope.

Parable: A short story that Jesus told to teach his apostles and followers.

Pastoral staff: Or crosier. Similar in appearance to a shepherd's crook, it is a sign of the governing office of a Bishop.

Penance: The recitation of a prayer, or performance of an act, imposed by a priest to a penitent in confession.

Penitential Rosary: Or Rosary of Padre Pio. One 'Our Father', one 'Hail Mary' and one 'Glory Be' are recited on **each** bead of the Rosary. It takes much longer to recite than the traditional Rosary.

Pope Gregory XVII: The self-appointed Pope of the Palmarian Church in Spain from 1978–2005.

Pope Paul VI: The elected Pope of the Roman Catholic Church from 1963–1978.

Pope Pius V: The elected Pope of the Roman Catholic Church from 1566–1572. He is important for his role in the Council of Trent, the Counter-Reformation, and the standardisation of the Roman Missal with the Tridentine or Latin Mass.

Presbytery: The residence or rectory of a priest.

Reading Souls: The ability to see into the heart and conscience of another human being, and to direct that person to a closer union with God.

Religious vocation: A 'calling' in the religious sense of the word which, if pursued, entails leaving home and family and dedicating one's life to God and His Church in a convent, monastery or priesthood.

Rosary: A devotion which focuses on meditating on the main events in the life of Jesus and Mary while reciting set prayers: one 'Our Father', ten 'Hail Marys', and one 'Glory be' constitute a decade. A Rosary is made up of five decades. There are three themes of meditation or 'Mysteries': the Joyful Mysteries which focus on the conception and birth of Jesus, the Sorrowful Mysteries about Jesus' death, and the Glorious Mysteries about His Resurrection.

Rosary beads: A string of beads used to count prayers in the recitation of the Rosary.

Rosary of Padre Pio of Pietrelcina: An extended version of the Rosary whereby one 'Our Father', one 'Hail Mary' and one 'Glory be' are recited on **each** bead.

Sacrament: An outward sign of inward grace. There are seven sacraments: Baptism, Confirmation, Penance, Holy Communion, Marriage, Holy Orders and Anointing of the Sick.

Saint Anthony of Padua: (1195–1231) A Franciscan friar. He is venerated throughout the world as the Patron Saint of lost articles. Many miracles have been attributed to him.

Saint Clare: (1194–1253) She founded the Poor Clares, a monastic Religious Order for women in the tradition of St Francis of Assisi.

Saint Francis of Assisi: (1181–1226) An Italian friar and preacher who founded the men's Order of Friars Minor. In 1224 he received the stigmata, making him the first recorded person to bear Christ's wounds in his body. He is the patron saint of animals.

Salvation: The saving of the soul from sin and its consequences, death, through personal effort and God's grace. Jesus' death on the cross is the ultimate sacrifice offered to God which atones for sin and ensures the possibility of salvation.

San Damiano, Italy: 1970s. Mama Rosa, a housewife, is reported to have had many visits from Our Lady in her garden at home, requesting a return to Catholic tradition, especially receiving Holy Communion on the tongue and not in the hand.

Sanctuary: An area at the front of a church near the tabernacle or altar. Altar rails sometimes mark the edge of the sanctuary.

Scapular – devotional: The devotional scapular can be worn by laypeople. It is a small piece of material, about an inch square, printed with religious images and attached to a cord worn around the neck. Throughout the centuries saints and popes have encouraged Catholics to wear the scapular with promises of special graces and eternal salvation. It serves to remind the wearer of their commitment to Christ.

Scapular – monastic: The monastic scapular, dating back to the seventh century, is worn by monks and nuns as part of their religious dress. It is a length of material suspended over the shoulders and flowing down the back and front.

Seminarian: A student of theology who is preparing for ordination to the priesthood.

Seminary: An institution or college for secondary or post-secondary education in theology for students preparing for the priesthood.

Shroud of Turin: A length of linen cloth bearing the image of a man who appears to have suffered crucifixion. It is believed by some to be the burial cloth of Jesus.

Sign of Peace: A handshake, hug or kiss that is exchanged during Mass after the Lord's Prayer but before Holy Communion. It signifies peace, communion and charity.

Six Commandments of the Church: Six laws considered binding by the Church which require believers to attend Mass, receive

Holy Communion, confess sins, fast, give alms, and observe the laws around marriage.

Sorrowful Mother: Or Our Lady of Sorrows. It refers to the sorrows she had to bear throughout her life.

Soutane: Or cassock. A full-length clerical garment traditionally worn by priests and buttoned down the front.

Stigmata: A term used to describe marks, sores, pains and wounds on the body in places that correspond to the five wounds of Jesus – hands/wrists, feet and side.

Surplice: A white liturgical garment, like a tunic, that reaches to the knees and has wide sleeves.

Tabernacle: A fixed, locked box-like vessel which resides in a church, usually on an altar, and houses the Blessed Eucharist, the consecrated Host.

The Trisagio: A prayer in honour of the Blessed Trinity.

The Way of the Cross: Or Stations of the Cross. They honour the events leading to Jesus' death.

Theology: The systematic and rational study of concepts of God and religious truths.

Transubstantiation: The change of the substance of the bread and wine into the Body and Blood of Christ – referring to what is changed, the substance, not how it occurs.

Tridentine Mass: The form of the Mass contained in the Roman Missal from 1570–1969 and usually celebrated in Latin.

Vatican Council II: (1962–1965) Or Vatican II. It was the twenty-first general council of the Catholic Church, and the biggest, with 2,600 bishops and 3,000 participants, including theologians and experts. It addressed relations between the Church and the modern world.

Made in the USA
Middletown, DE
25 July 2018